RENEWING
THE WORLD

RENEWING
THE WORLD

A Concise Global History of
the Stone-Campbell Movement

GARY HOLLOWAY and

DOUGLAS A. FOSTER

Abilene Christian University Press

RENEWING THE WORLD

A Concise Global History of the Stone-Campbell Movement

Copyright © 2015 by Gary Holloway and Douglas A. Foster

ISBN 978-0-89112-373-6

Printed in the United States of America

Drawing of James O'Kelly, page 19, courtesy of Special Collections Department, Elon University

Photos on pages 167, 169, courtesy of Southeast Christian Church

Cover design by Jennette Munger

For information contact:
Abilene Christian University Press
ACU Box 29138
Abilene, Texas 79699

1-877-816-4455
www.acupressbooks.com

To the World Convention of Churches of Christ
that exists to cooperate with Christians everywhere
toward the unity of the Church.

Contents

Preface

There are churches from what historians call the Stone-Campbell Movement in 199 countries with over 10 million adherents. Though known by various names— Churches of Christ, Christians, Disciples—these churches have much in common.

One thing they have in common is a serious lack of knowledge of their past and an increasing desire by many to know more of their heritage. This desire has led us to believe there is a need for a brief account of the history of these churches globally. This book hopes to serve both newcomers and long-time members of those churches by giving them insights into our heritage. It also serves as an introduction to this significant group of churches for those unfamiliar with its place in global Christianity.

Looking at one's spiritual ancestry is as pleasurable and painful as examining one's family tree. Some ancestors and family stories make us swell with pride, while others we would just as soon forget. As two insiders to the Stone-Campbell Movement, we write with a deep appreciation for those who have gone before us. We would in no way bash the church of our mothers and fathers. As serious historians, however, we present our story as we see it, "warts and all."

Thus, as we look forward to God's future blessings on this movement, we also look back to how God has led us kindly in the past and how we have followed or resisted. This book is not a collection of interesting trivia—though we do hope it will be interesting. Instead, we hope our work will provide us a usable past. There are marvelous aspects to our tradition that we need to recover today and lessons that we must learn as we continually reform and conform the church to the image of Christ.

This has been in every way a joint project. As we worked on this book together, we have learned the difficulties and the joys of Christian unity. We have not always agreed, but we have always been willing to discuss. This seems to us the basis for more than writing together. It reflects the attitude toward Christian unity modeled by those studied in this book.

This book is a concise history, which means we had to select only a few of the stories we could have and told them briefly. The stories of many other servants of Christ from all over the world deserve to be told, but we could not tell them. Many other stories are told in two larger works on which this book depends—*The Encyclopedia of the Stone-Campbell Movement* (Eerdmans, 2004), edited by Douglas A. Foster, D. Newell Williams, Paul M. Blowers, and Anthony L. Dunnavant, and *The Stone-Campbell Movement: A Global History* (Chalice, 2013), also edited by Foster, Williams, and Blowers. This book is the fourth in a series of concise histories of Stone-Campbell movement churches published by Leafwood Publishers. Previous volumes are *Renewing God's People: A Concise History of Churches of Christ* (2001), *Renewal for Mission: A Concise History of Christian Churches and Churches of Christ* (2009), and *Renewing Christian Unity: A Concise History of the Christian Church (Disciples of Christ)* (2011).

One difficulty in writing this concise global history is finding accurate statistics for these churches worldwide. In keeping with standard practice, we have generally given the numbers of adherents (members and children). We have relied primarily on three sources for these locations and numbers—the profiles of our churches compiled for the World Convention by Clinton J. Holloway (see http://www.worldconvention.org/resources/profiles/), the numbers in the World Christian Database (see http://www.worldchristiandatabase.org/wcd/), and statistics from sources like Missions Resource Network (see http://www.mrnet.org/taxonomy/term/786).

Do We Have A History?

Those in the Stone-Campbell Movement have mixed feelings about our history. Indeed, some would deny that we have a history. They say things like, "Aren't we the church of the first century? Isn't all church history after the first century just a record of apostasy and corruption? Shouldn't we leap over those years to the purity of the early church? Don't we undercut our plea to be biblical by admitting we have a history? Shouldn't we deny or at least downplay our particular history to be unified with all Christians?"

MANY BIRTHDAYS

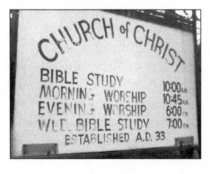

We understand those who want to deny our history. On the side of the church building where one of us grew up were the words: "Church of Christ, Established 33 A.D." The idea was that we wanted to be the church of the New Testament, the one established at Pentecost. That ideal still burns brightly in many hearts in this heritage. We cannot and do not want to restore everything about the early church (no one wants to be exactly like the Corinthians), but we do want to be the kind of church that the first century churches should have been. In a real sense, we like all Christians can trace our existence to that first church at Pentecost.

But do we have a history after Pentecost? Honesty requires that we answer, "Yes." The history of the whole church, as messy and fallen as it has been, is our history. Although we want to be like the early church, we must admit that we are not the first Christians. Two thousand years have past. Previous generations have passed the faith on to us. We would not have the Bible itself were it not for the faithful labors of copyists and translators. One reason for studying church history is to honor our spiritual mothers and fathers.

Studying church history also helps us experience how faithful Christians in the past struggled to follow God in their own context. If we can see how the church in the past often conformed to parts of its culture that were contrary to the gospel, then perhaps we can see how parts of our own culture threaten to subvert today's church. Studying church history may also show how the church has shaped the culture around it in positive ways.

Studying history can also help us understand the Bible. We prize the authority of the Bible because those who went before us taught us to respect it. By seeing how previous generations understood (and misunderstood) the Bible, we gain a perspective on its meaning for our time.

Although a number of independent reform movements in Britain and North America preceded and eventually fed into the Stone-Campbell Movement in the United States, this book begins with a focus on our history in the context of America. While it is true in one sense that Pentecost is our birthday, there are other dates to which we can point as beginning points of the Stone-Campbell Movement. The first "founding document" of our immediate history is *The Last Will and Testament of the Springfield Presbytery* written in 1804. The ministers who wrote those words began the first group of churches in this movement. Although many before him called Christians back to the Bible for the sake of Christian unity, Thomas Campbell's publication of *The Declaration and Address* in 1809 marked a significant intellectual beginning to this movement. In the past, many in America saw that date as the movement's starting point. Disciples celebrated the centennial of Campbell's call for unity in 1909, and members of the Stone-Campbell Movement around the world celebrated the bicentennial in 2009.

At the end of the nineteenth century, the Movement in North America divided with Disciples of Christ (or Christian Churches) and Churches of Christ becoming separate groups. Some place that division in 1889, when Daniel Sommer and others called for a break of fellowship in the "Address and Declaration" at Sand Creek, Illinois. A more "official" marker of that division was recorded in the U.S. Census of Religious Bodies in 1906. In North America, a second division resulted in the separation of Christian Churches/ Churches of Christ and the Christian Church (Disciples of Christ), often marked by the Disciples "restructure" in 1968.

Around the world others celebrate yet other dates marking when the Stone-Campbell Movement began in their countries.

So what is our birthday? All and none of the above. We do want to be the church founded at the first Pentecost after the resurrection of Jesus. Yet, we must admit that we are the church in a particular context, shaped by Paul, Peter, Augustine, Teresa, Luther, Calvin, Wesley, Thomas Campbell, Alexander Campbell, Barton Stone, and countless others.

TRADITION AND TRADITIONALISM

In our formative years, churches from the Stone-Campbell Movement had (and many continue to have) a strong opposition to "tradition." This opposition raises the question, "Why should we study our history if we have always been against tradition?" The answer lies in the distinction between "tradition" and "traditionalism." Historian Jaroslav Pelikan has defined tradition as "the living faith of the dead," and traditionalism as "the dead faith of the living."

The Bible is both positive and negative about tradition (the biblical word means simply "something passed down"). When tradition becomes traditionalism, that is, when it takes the place of the original intent of God, then it deserves condemnation. Both

13

Jesus (Matthew 15:1–6) and Paul (Colossians 2:8) condemn human traditions that supersede the will of God. On the other hand, Paul many times urges the churches to "hold on to the traditions" he had taught them (I Corinthians 11:2; 2 Thessalonians 2:15; 3:6). These were not mere human traditions, but beliefs and practices handed down from Christ and the apostles.

So, why study the history of the Stone-Campbell Movement? To honor our spiritual ancestors who passed the tradition of the faith on to us. Traditions must always be subject to the authority of Scripture; indeed, one of our strongest traditions is the ultimate authority of the Bible over tradition! Nevertheless, traditions are inevitable. They give shape to our church life and help in passing on the faith. The alternative would be starting the church over again every day, which would result in chaos. Those traditions become harmful only when they change into fixed traditionalism that leads us away from the intent of Scripture.

In other words, denying we have a history leads to danger. Failure to recognize that our history shapes us results in our being prisoners to it. By being blind to the historical forces that shape our church practices, we fall prey to the danger of mistaking our circumstances and conclusions with the eternal will of God. By denying we have a history, we easily become traditionalists like the Pharisees who equated their teachings with God's Word.

We write this brief history as committed members of churches of the Stone-Campbell Movement. If we deny the good our spiritual ancestors accomplished, we become ungrateful children. If we ignore their mistakes, we become traditionalists who prize our own human history above the will of God. If we fail to understand that we have been profoundly shaped by the people, ideas and events that came before us, we risk seeing everything we do as simply "what the Bible says." Only by looking honestly at who we have been can we understand who we are, and who God is shaping us to be. God has given us the ability to think historically and to grow in our understanding through the powerful gift of a sense of history. Using that gift is part of being faithful to God in our time and place, part of our spiritual formation.

CHAPTER 1

The Promise of Restoration in Early America

What characteristics of American Christianity proved so advantageous to the rise and phenomenal growth of the Stone-Campbell Movement in the United States in the early 1800s? The answer to this question is rooted in the history of America. Although most of the early English colonies in America had established, tax-supported religions, a new situation developed in Colonial America that had never existed before. No single religious group gained political control over all the colonies. The Puritans dominated New England, but there were also Baptists and Anglicans there. The Anglicans were most numerous in the southern colonies, but there were also Presbyterians and Methodists. The middle colonies had the greatest religious diversity with Quakers, Lutherans, German Reformed, Baptists, Anglicans, and others.

Consequently, no one denomination could be *the* church of America. Americans take that situation for granted today, but it was unique for its time. In Europe, every country had an official state religion, with (at best) limited tolerance for other religious groups. For example, English authorities jailed the Separatist Puritans we call the "Pilgrims" for preaching against the Church of England. Therefore, they left England for the Netherlands and eventually came to America, not to find the religious freedom we have today, but to have the freedom to set up "the true church" as they saw it. They were no more tolerant of Quakers and Baptists than the English authorities had been tolerant of Puritans.

A NEW VIEW OF RELIGIOUS FREEDOM

Since no religious group dominated all the colonies, a new form of religious freedom developed in America. It was a freedom from church or clerical authority. Reflecting the love of liberty ingrained in the American mind by the Revolution, many in the United States, especially on the frontier, wanted no part of a Pope, a bishop, or even a group of clergy making rules for the church. Instead, they longed for a more democratic form of government where ordinary members made collective decisions for the church. This desire for religious democracy also produced a new form of minister—one who was not formally educated, but who came from the people—in contrast to the older elite, educated ministry.

American religious freedom was also a freedom from tradition. For many American churches, the common sense of the people replaced the rulings of Popes and councils, the historic creeds, and the writings of educated theologians. The people should read the Bible and think for themselves, not trust the clergy to do their thinking for them.

Because of this democratization of Christianity, another freedom arose—the freedom to begin new churches without government restrictions. What happened if your reading of Scripture differed significantly from the teaching of your church? If you could not persuade your church to change, then there was no choice left but to form your own "true" church. As a result, dozens of upstart churches began and prospered in America, including a variety of Methodist, Baptist and "Christian" groups, some eventually outgrowing the more established churches. Over time, however, those newer churches themselves resisted change in their practices and grew to be prominent in the larger culture. Consequently, some in those groups rebelled against their tradition and formed still other religious sects.

A NEW VIEW OF RELIGIOUS AUTHORITY

Because of this freedom, many thought it no longer necessary for religious authority to come from a recognized hierarchy, creeds, and educated clergy. Instead it became truly democratic, a rule of the people. The Reformation principle of *sola scriptura* (Scripture alone) evolved into the idea that each Christian was his or her own interpreter of the Bible.

This interpretation was profoundly shaped by a specific kind of rationalism and common sense philosophy. Human reason was to judge the truth of all religious teaching. Increasingly, this meant that each individual had the right and responsibility to read Scripture and interpret it. However, personal experience shaped this rationalism, particularly on the American frontier. In other words, true religion was to be heart-felt and mysterious, while at the same time being reasonable to the average person.

Ironically, this rejection of traditional religious authorities gave power to another elite— religious demagogues. Although theoretically each person was a Bible interpreter, in fact a religious leader who could move an audience had tremendous influence on how that audience read Scripture. This accounts for the rise of popular preaching in the language of the people. It also explains the popularity of the new religious press. By publishing a paper, preachers could move thousands to see the Bible and the church their way. Popular hymns also shaped the theology of the people.

As many Americans rejected traditional religious authority to appeal to the authority of personal interpretation of Scripture, it left them with the uncertain authority of popular preachers and mass movements. Denominations multiplied. The church was visibly less unified. Religious truth often became a product of "the people" in a destructive way. For some, numbers became the authentication of their faithfulness. Too often, freedom to follow Scripture for one's self became bondage to self-promoting preachers who could sway the most people.

A CALL FOR RESTORATION

This was the setting for the birth of the Stone-Campbell Movement. Many were looking for a more sure authority in religion. They wondered why there were so many denominations and which (if any) was the true church. The scandal of division among Christians was especially evident on the frontier. A small settlement of a hundred people might have three or more struggling churches, often in constant conflict with each other over who was the true church.

But the United States also offered religious leaders the freedom to rethink the shape of the church. In this atmosphere, many decided that a return to the Bible and the church of the New Testament offered the best hope of having a faithful and a unified church in their new American setting. These "back to the Bible" movements grew up in several denominations in various parts of the nation.

The dream of going "back to the Bible" did not begin in eighteenth century America. The Renaissance call to go "back to the sources" led many like the Roman Catholic scholar Erasmus (1466–1536) to emphasize the importance of going to the New Testament for guidance and authority. The Reformation had its motto of *sola scriptura*, Scripture alone. The Puritans in England and the early New England colonies wanted their churches to resemble closely the biblical model.

In eighteenth-century Britain as well, a few began to call for a more radical "restoration" of New Testament Christianity. Groups like the Haldanes and Glasites broke from the Church of Scotland—which was itself a "Puritan" Presbyterian church— to undertake a more thorough purification than could be done under a state church. These ideas would have an even more extensive influence on American religious leaders, who began calling for a more thorough reformation of the church, some also using the word "restoration." What exactly did they mean by "Restoration Movement"?

The underlying concept was that important teachings and practices that were to characterize Christ's church in all times and places had been lost or obscured through the centuries. Anabaptists at the time of the Protestant Reformation had articulated this idea strongly and other "radicals" had adopted it. Though different groups saw different things that needed restoring, all focused on bringing back vital beliefs and practices they believed the church no longer had. One metaphor for this renewal of the church is restoring a house. Restoring the church was not building from scratch; it's not as though the church had disappeared, but it had deteriorated through the years and needed to be restored to its original state. Essential portions of the house may be sound and original—the foundation and plumbing, for example—while other portions need replacing. Alexander Campbell saw his purpose as bringing "Christianity and the church up to the New Testament standard."

Restoration was the goal of all the groups in this chapter. What most also had in common was agreement on the purpose of restoration. To be the pure church of the Bible was not an end in itself. The purpose of restoring the church was to reach the visible unity among Christians that Christ prayed for, "That all of them may be one . . . so that the world might believe" (John 17:21). Although there were significant differences among these groups, they all called Christians back to the Bible to restore to the church things they believed it had lost and that would make the church what it was truly meant to be.

CHRISTIANS OF THE SOUTH: JAMES O'KELLY

"I am for Bible government, Christian equality, and the Christian name." So said James O'Kelly (1735–1826), an early Methodist preacher in North Carolina and Virginia. When the Methodist church in America organized in Baltimore in 1784, O'Kelly and a few other ministers questioned the appointment of Francis Asbury as one of two superintendents of the church. They believed Asbury, who began to call himself bishop, held too much power over the churches. Eventually, O'Kelly not only opposed Asbury but the whole idea of a bishop who appoints ministers in each church. Instead, he felt each

James O'Kelly

congregation should act democratically, like a republic, to govern its own affairs.

In 1793, O'Kelly and others broke from Asbury's leadership, calling themselves Republican Methodists. In August 1794, the leaders of this group met and went one step farther. They decided to use the name "Christians" to the exclusion of other names and take the Bible alone as their creed.

Eventually, they adopted five "Cardinal Principles of the Christian Church."

1. The Lord Jesus Christ is the only Head of the Church.
2. The name Christian should be used to the exclusion of all party and sectarian names.
3. The Holy Bible, or Scriptures of the Old and New Testaments, is our only creed, and a sufficient rule of faith and practice.
4. Christian character, or vital piety, is the only test of church fellowship and membership.
5. The right of private judgment and the liberty of conscience are the privilege and duty of all.

These leaders did not intend these items as a formal creed (since item three rejects creeds), but these propositions do express the basic outlook of the O'Kelly group and of all the new restoration movements in America. Note that even Christian unity was not an end in itself, but was for the purpose of the evangelism of the world.

These Christian churches eventually numbered around 10,000 members in North Carolina and Virginia. Some of these congregations eventually adopted believer's immersion and united with the New England Christians in the early 1800s (see below). Others maintained infant baptism and rejoined the Methodists in 1934. Others joined with the Stone "Christians" (see chapter two). One connection between the O'Kelly and the Stone Movements was the work of Rice Haggard (1769–1819) who convinced both groups to take the name "Christian" to the exclusion of other names.

THE NEW ENGLAND CHRISTIANS: ABNER JONES AND ELIAS SMITH

Independently a similar Movement arose among Baptists in New England. At this time, Baptists were strongly Calvinistic, believing in predestination. Abner Jones (1772–1841), a physician and preacher in Vermont, joined with like-minded Baptists in denying Calvinism and taking the name Christian. They organized a Christian church in Lyndon, Vermont, in 1801. Jones became a traveling evangelist, spreading the message of non-creedal Christianity.

In 1803, Jones met Elias Smith (1769–1846), another Baptist minister who had formed a Christian congregation the previous year in Portsmouth, New Hampshire. Smith was a fiery proponent of religious freedom who published one of the earliest Christian papers in America, the *Herald of Gospel Liberty* (begun in 1808). He also popularized his ideas through hymns that attacked the prevailing religious authorities. Jones and Smith combined their efforts and by 1807 had established fourteen congregations of Christians in New England.

The Smith-Jones Movement was so insistent on doctrinal diversity that eventually it splintered and disappeared as a separate fellowship. Some became Unitarians; many later joined the Adventists. Some joined with the O'Kelly Christians in the South and the Stone Movement to form the Christian Connection. In 1931, the congregations of the Connection that had not united with the Campbell Movement in the nineteenth century became part of the Congregational Christian Church, which in turn merged with the Evangelical and Reformed Church to form the United Church of Christ in 1957.

Elias Smith

The religious freedom available in the United States thus produced two Christian "restoration" movements, one from the Methodists and

21

one from the Baptists. It was to produce two more from a Presbyterian background.

QUESTIONS FOR DISCUSSION

1. What factors led to religious freedom in America? How does that freedom help explain the unique aspects of American religion?

2. Why are there so many different churches in America? Why have new religious groups been so popular in the United States?

3. What do you first think of when you hear "Restoration Movement"? How have many in the Stone-Campbell Movement understood restoration? How should we understand it?

4. Is visible Christian unity still a noble goal to pursue? What would that unity look like?

5. Are the "five points" of the O'Kelly Christians a good summary of what the church should be? What would you add or subtract from their list?

6. What did the Smith-Jones New England Christians and the O'Kelly Christians have in common? How were they different? What can we learn today from these two groups?

FOR FURTHER READING

Foster, Douglas A., Newell Williams, Paul M. Blowers, and Anthony L. Dunnavant, eds. *The Encyclopedia of the Stone-Campbell Movement*. Grand Rapids, Michigan: Eerdmans, 2004. See articles on Christian Connection; Jones, Abner; New England "Christians"; O'Kelly, James; and Smith, Elias.

Allen, J. Timothy. "Some Expectation of Being Promoted: Ambition, Abolition, and the Reverend James O'Kelly," *North Carolina Historical Review* 84, 1 (January 2007): 59–81.

Conkin, Paul K. *American Originals.* Chapel Hill: University of North Carolina Press, 1997. See pages 1–8.

Garrett, Leroy. *The Stone-Campbell Movement.* Joplin, Missouri: College Press, 1994. See pages 47–70.

Hatch, Nathan O. "The Christian Movement and the Demand for a Theology of the People," *American Origins of Churches of Christ.* Abilene, Texas: Abilene Christian University Press, 2000. See pages 11–44.

Hatch, Nathan O. *The Democratization of American Christianity.* New Haven: Yale University Press, 1989.

Olbricht, Thomas. "Christian Connexion and Unitarian relations 1800–1844" *Restoration Quarterly* 9, 3 (1966): 160–186.

Website

Disciples of Christ Historical Society. http://www.discipleshistory.org/.

CHAPTER

2

Barton Stone and Christian Unity

A
lthough there were groups of "Christians" in the South and in
New England, the largest bodies grew out of Presbyterian and
Baptist churches in Kentucky and Tennessee. The leader of these
"Christians of the West" was a deeply spiritual man named Barton
W. Stone.

STONE'S EARLY LIFE

Barton W. Stone (1772–1844) was born in Maryland and raised as
a nominal Episcopalian. In 1779, after the death of his father, Stone
moved with his family to Virginia. During his teen years, he occa-
sionally heard preaching from Baptist and Methodist ministers, but
was not impressed with their message or personal lives. He decided
to improve his position in society by continuing his education and
becoming a lawyer.

He enrolled in a "log college," a typical, one-teacher frontier
school, run by David Caldwell (1725–1824), a Presbyterian minister in North Carolina. Under his influence and the preaching of
revivalist James McGready (1760–1817), Stone had a conversion
experience, became a Presbyterian, and felt the call to preach.
Finishing his studies with Caldwell in three years, Stone would
have been one of the most educated persons on the American
frontier.

Stone had many internal struggles before he was ordained as
a Presbyterian minister. He questioned the depth of his conversion,
the genuineness of his call to preach, and the truth of the traditional

Barton W. Stone

doctrines of the Trinity and predestination. He believed so strongly in the reality of but one God, that the idea of the Trinity even disrupted his prayer life. For a while he taught at a Methodist school in Georgia, but soon made a trek across Tennessee and Kentucky in 1796, preaching and searching for God's will for his life.

Stone eventually concluded God had called him to preach and so sought ordination from the Presbyterian Church in the Transylvania Presbytery at Cane Ridge, Kentucky, where he had been preaching for two years. He still had serious doubts about the doctrine of the Trinity found in the Westminster Confession of Faith (the basic creed of the Presbyterians). Agreement with this Presbyterian confession was required for ordination. After some discussion with the presbytery, he was asked if he would adopt the Confession of Faith. He replied, "I do, as far as I see it consistent with the word of God." This reply was common among those trained in the revival tradition in Presbyterianism, and so satisfied the presbytery. Thus Stone was ordained and assigned to minister to the churches at Cane Ridge and Concord, Kentucky, in 1798.

THE CANE RIDGE REVIVAL

In August 1801, Stone's Cane Ridge church was the site of the largest and most famous "camp meeting" revival in American history. A wave of revivals led by James McGready and others had broken out in southern Kentucky in 1800. At the Cane Ridge revival, crowds estimated from ten to thirty thousand heard Presbyterian, Methodist, and Baptist ministers preach repentance. During their preaching, many listeners experienced what Stone and

26

others called "religious exercises." Some fell to the ground in a faint as if they were dead. Many jerked back and forth, sometimes making a sound like a bark. Others felt the bodily agitations coming upon them and tried to run away. Some danced rhythmically back and forth until they dropped from exhaustion. A few laughed a hearty, solemn laugh.

Does this make Stone Pentecostal or Charismatic? No. In his autobiography Stone attributed the "exercises" to the "circumstances of the times." Many people had come to expect Christ's second coming and the end of the world to be very soon. Events like the Napoleonic Wars, the massive earthquake that created a new lake between Kentucky and Tennessee just a couple of years earlier, and comets seen streaking across the sky were interpreted to be signs of the end of time. This heightened expectation and even fear was undoubtedly behind the large crowds that flowed to Cane Ridge and the revivals before it. The tensions created by the preaching and exhorting day after day, the emotional singing, the calls for repentance and coming to Christ, when added to the already intense anxiety about the end of the world, produced, in Stone's view, the eccentric actions seen at Cane Ridge.

The sanctuary that now shelters the Cane Ridge Meetinghouse

Still, while he thought the exercises at Cane Ridge were a product of the circumstances of the times, he believed all his life that the Holy Spirit had worked on people in the midst of the exercises to bring them to Christ. Such physical manifestations were certainly not to be the universal experience of all Christians. Yet he believed that God's Holy Spirit can work in the hearts of people in any circumstances to "get their attention" and help them hear and accept the good news of the gospel of Jesus Christ. Stone was never afraid of such manifestations. He believed God worked in many ways to draw people to the gospel. To call him Pentecostal or Charismatic would be inaccurate and anachronistic.

The Cane Ridge Revival had a profound effect on Stone and others. It convinced them of the importance of Christian unity. If the Spirit could work through Presbyterian, Methodist and Baptist preaching, then the differences between these denominations must not be matters of the gospel. The unity among Christians produced by God's Spirit should be a goal of all who claim to follow Christ. In Stone's later words, "Let Christian unity be our polar star."

The experiences of Cane Ridge also increased the doubts that Stone and his fellow ministers had about Calvinistic predestination. Although one can be a Calvinist and a revivalist, they had seen many freely respond to the gospel during the revivals. They felt more at home with a doctrine of limited but real free will.

The Last Will and Testament

This desire for unity soon proved itself in concrete action. The Presbyterian Synod of Kentucky questioned Stone and five other ministers about their support of the revival, their more open stance toward other Christians, and their doubts about Calvinism. Before the Synod could discipline them, they broke away and formed their own association, the Springfield Presbytery. Within a year, however, they decided the Springfield Presbytery itself worked against biblical unity so they disbanded. They explained their reasons in *The Last Will and Testament of the Springfield Presbytery* written in 1804. This document is so significant in our history that we reproduce most of it here, including its nineteenth century grammar and style:

The PRESBYTERY OF SPRINGFIELD, sitting at Cane-ridge, in the county of Bourbon, being, through a gracious Providence, in more than ordinary bodily health, growing in strength and size daily; and in perfect soundness and composure of mind; but knowing that it is appointed for all delegated bodies once to die: and considering that the life of every such body is very uncertain, do make, and ordain this our Last Will and Testament, in manner and form following, viz.:

Imprimis. We *will,* that this body die, be dissolved, and sink into union with the Body of Christ at large; for there is but one body, and one spirit, even as we are called in one hope of our calling.

Item. We *will,* that our name of distinction, with its *Reverend* title, be forgotten, that there be but one Lord over God's heritage, and his name one.

Item. We *will,* that our power of making laws for the government of the church, and executing them by del-egated authority, forever cease; that the people may have free course to the Bible, and adopt *the law of the spirit of life in Christ Jesus.*

Item. We *will,* that candidates for the Gospel ministry henceforth study the Holy Scriptures with fervent prayer, and obtain license from God to preach the simple Gospel, *with the Holy Ghost sent down from heaven,* without any mixture of philosophy, vain deceit, traditions of men, or the rudiments of the world. And let none henceforth take *this honor to himself, but he that is called of God, as was Aaron.*

Item. We *will,* that the church of Christ assume her native right of internal government—try her candidates for the ministry, as to their soundness in the faith, acquaintance with experimental religion, gravity and aptness to teach; and admit no other proof of their authority but Christ speaking in them. We will that the church of Christ look up to the Lord of the harvest to send forth labourers into his harvest; and that she resume her primitive right of trying those *who say they are Apostles, and are not.*

Item. We *will,* that each particular church, as a body, actuated by the same spirit, choose her own preacher, and support him by a free will offering, without written *call* or *subscription*—admit members—remove offences; and never henceforth *delegate* her right of government to any man or set of men whatever.

Item. We *will,* that the people henceforth take the Bible as the only sure guide to heaven; and as many as are offended with other books, which stand in competition with it, may cast them into the fire if they choose: for it is better to enter into life having one book, than having many to be cast into hell.

Item. We *will,* that preachers and people, cultivate a spirit of mutual forbearance; pray more and dispute less; and while they behold the signs of the times, look up, and confidently expect that redemption draweth nigh.

Item. We *will,* that our weak brethren, who may have been wishing to make the Presbytery of Springfield their king, and wot not what is now become of it, betake them-selves to the Rock of Ages, and follow Jesus for the future.

Item. We *will,* that the Synod of Kentucky examine every member, who may be *suspected* of having departed from the Confession of Faith, and suspend every such sus-pected heretic immediately; in order that the oppressed may go free, and taste the sweets of gospel liberty.

Item. Finally we *will,* that all our *sister bodies* read their Bibles carefully, that they may see their fate there determined, and prepare for death before it is too late.

Signed by Stone and five other ministers, this was a clear call for restoration and unity. Much of this document still has influence on the churches of the Stone-Campbell Movement. Some items deserve to have more influence. Christians should follow the Bible alone. Each local congregation should run its own affairs and choose its own ministers, who are to be ordained with authority and responsibility, but not to be rule-making "reverends." There should be no formal authoritative organization beyond the local church, such as a presbytery or general assembly. A spirit of cooperation and freedom should prevail. We should pray more and dispute less, prayerfully looking forward to the redemption Christ will bring at his Second Coming.

THE GROWTH OF THE STONE MOVEMENT

At the suggestion of Rice Haggard, a former associate of James O'Kelly, Stone and his followers soon called themselves Christians and established congregations they called Churches of Christ or Christian Churches. By 1807, the question of baptism arose in the Movement. Eventually the Stone churches practiced believer's immersion but did not make it an absolute test of fellowship (those baptized as infants could still be members and commune). Stone feared that making believer's immersion a test of fellowship would exclude more Christians than any creed.

Stone faced vehement opposition to two of his theological positions. He denied the substitutionary view of the atonement, the idea that Christ paid our debt to God on the cross. To Stone, such a view made God a hateful tyrant demanding payment instead of a loving Father. He also would not affirm the traditional doctrine of the Trinity although he did praise Jesus as the Son of God and Savior. On these issues, Stone insisted on the literal wording of the Bible, accusing others of speculative theology.

Yet in spite of Stone's theological opponents, the defection of some leaders to the Shakers, and the return of others to the Presbyterians, by the 1820s the Stone Movement had grown to twelve thousand members and spread from Kentucky and Ohio to Tennessee, Alabama, Missouri, and Illinois. A great deal of this growth was due to whole congregations of Separate Baptists giving up their "Baptist" name to be "Christians."

This growth was also the result of the example and character of Barton W. Stone. Not only was he a tireless evangelist, but his peaceful spirit and love for the lost influenced others through his paper, *The Christian Messenger* (published 1826–1844). Although Stone continued to discuss his objections to substitutionary atonement and traditional Trinitarianism in his paper, he focused more often on Christian tolerance and unity. Soon he would make his unity teaching concrete by promoting the union of the churches of his movement with those of a movement led by Thomas and Alexander Campbell.

Thus by 1804 there were three independent movements in America attempting to be "Christians only." Although there were differences among them, having come from three different denominations—Methodists, Baptists, and Presbyterians—their similarities are striking. All three wanted the Bible alone to be their creed. All took the name "Christian." All organized congregationally, without the control of a bishop or a clergy-led presbytery. Each worked to promote visible Christian unity. All were evangelistic. These "restoration movements" were to have a lasting heritage in America.

QUESTIONS FOR DISCUSSION

1. How would you explain the "spiritual exercises" at the Cane Ridge Revival? Were these genuine experiences of the Holy Spirit, or should they be explained another way? Is there room in your church for such experiences today? Should there be?

2. List and discuss at least five themes found in *The Last Will and Testament of the Springfield Presbytery* that still influence your church. What else can we learn from this document to help our current spiritual walk?

3. Why might Stone object to the idea of substitutionary atonement, that Jesus paid our debt of sin to alleviate God's anger toward us? What does this doctrine imply about God?

4. How important is the doctrine of the Trinity? How important has it been in churches of the Stone-Campbell Movement?

5. What are the similarities and differences among the three "Christian" groups we have discussed so far?

For Further Reading

Foster, Douglas A., Newell Williams, Paul M. Blowers, and Anthony L. Dunnavant, eds. *The Encyclopedia of the Stone-Campbell Movement.* Grand Rapids, Michigan: Eerdmans, 2004. See articles on Cane Ridge Meeting House; Cane Ridge Revival; Springfield Presbytery; Stone, Barton Warren.

Newell, Williams, Douglas Foster, and Paul Blowers. *The Stone-Campbell Movement: A Global History.* St. Louis, Missouri: Chalice 2013. See pages 9–16.

Conkin, Paul K. *American Originals.* Chapel Hill: University of North Carolina Press, 1997. See pages 8–14.

Garrett, Leroy. *The Stone-Campbell Movement.* Joplin, Missouri: College Press, 1994. See pages 71–95.

Williams, D. Newell. *Barton Stone, A Spiritual Biography.* St Louis: Chalice Press, 2000.

CHAPTER 3

The Coming of the Campbells

While O'Kelly, Smith, Jones, and Stone were forming Christian groups in America, Thomas Campbell (1763–1854) was still in Ireland. The religious pilgrimage of the Campbell family is interesting. Thomas's father, Archibald Campbell, was an Anglican converted from Roman Catholicism. Thomas converted to the Presbyterian Church of Scotland, becoming a minister for the Ahorey Church in Rich Hill, Ireland.

While in Ireland, Thomas Campbell became dissatisfied with the narrowness of the Old Light, Anti-Burgher, Seceder Presbyterian Church to which he belonged. Each of these terms denoted a previous doctrinal split among the Presbyterians. Campbell longed instead for the unity he believed the early church enjoyed and even made several unsuccessful attempts to unite the different factions in the Seceder Church in Ireland. These failures contributed to serious physical illness and a growing desire to move to a place where such divisions would not exist.

In 1807, Thomas came to America, leaving his family behind in Ireland to join him later. Assigned by his church (the Associate Synod of North America) to preach in Western Pennsylvania, Campbell soon was in trouble for allowing Presbyterians not of his faction to take the Lord's Supper. Censured by his presbytery and synod, Campbell and a number of sympathizers began an inter-denominational group, patterned on British missionary and Bible societies, known as the Christian Association of Washington, Pennsylvania.

DECLARATION AND ADDRESS

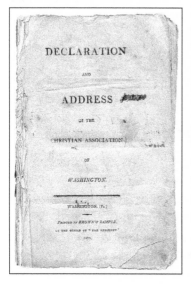

In 1809, the Christian Association commissioned Thomas Campbell to write a document outlining the purpose of the organization and its plan for unity among Christians. This *Declaration and Address* (a reference to the freedom proclaimed by the American *Declaration of Independence*) made a clear call back to the freedom found in the New Testament as a basis for Christian unity.

A much longer and more complex document than the *Last Will and Testament of Springfield Presbytery*, the main points of the *Declaration and Address* include:

1. *A fervent call to Christian unity.* "That the Church of Christ on earth is essentially, intentionally, and constitutionally one." It is one in essence because Christians are "subjects of the same grace, objects of the same divine love, bought with the same price, and joint heirs of the same inheritance." God intends the church to be one, evidenced by Jesus' fervent prayer for unity in John 17. The "constitution" that makes the church one is the New Testament.

2. *A strong condemnation of division among Christians.* "That division among Christians is a horrid evil, fraught with many evils." Thus, there should "be no schisms, no uncharitable divisions among them."

3. *Doctrinal differences not based on the express teachings of the New Testament are the causes of division.* More than sixty times in the *Declaration and Address*, Campbell uses phrases like "expressly exhibited," "plain," and "clear"

to describe the binding teachings of Scripture. Where the Bible is unclear or silent, no disagreement should divide Christians. Thomas Campbell never spelled out exactly what those "express teachings" are. Neither does he address the difficulty of Christians strongly disagreeing over what the Bible "expressly" teaches. This would be a significant problem later in the Campbell Movement.

4. *A simple confession of faith in Jesus, not agreement with an elaborate creed, is all that is necessary for admission to the church.* Thus, creeds, even if true and helpful, should not be used to exclude Christians who disagree with them from full acceptance as children of God.

5. *A desire to return to the purity of the first century church.* By removing items he believed had divided Christians and obscured the beauty of the church, God's people could experience personal and corporate holiness and purity.

6. *An appeal for love and understanding among Christians.* Those who confess faith in Christ "should consider each other as the precious saints of God, should love each other as brethren, children of the same family and Father, temples of the same Spirit, members of the same body . . . ."

Thomas Campbell never intended the principles of the *Declaration and Address* to be the basis of a new religious group. Instead, it was a call to unity among Christians of all denominations. "The cause that we advocate is not our own peculiar cause, nor the cause of any party, considered as such; it is a common cause, the cause of Christ and our brethren of all denominations."

Most Christians around them, however, rejected the appeal of the

Thomas Campbell

37

Christian Association, so the group eventually formed the nucleus of a new congregation, the Brush Run church. By forming a church, Campbell made his quest for Christian unity more difficult. Even today, in a Bible study group with people from different denominations, it seems as if we have so much in common. Why can't we unite? But if that Bible study group were to become a church, then they would have to make decisions that would highlight the differences among them. How will they worship? Who will lead them? Who can be a part of this church? What does the church believe and teach? It is easier to talk about unity than to reach it.

Having said this, we don't want to diminish the power of Thomas Campbell's call to Christian unity. The *Declaration and Address* reminds us that if we are to be biblical we must make unity a priority as Christ did in his dying prayer.

ALEXANDER CAMPBELL IN SCOTLAND

The rest of Thomas Campbell's family, including his oldest son Alexander (1788–1866), soon boarded a ship from Ireland to join him in America. After storms shipwrecked it off the coast of Scotland, the family spent close to a year in Glasgow, 1808–1809, allowing Alexander to attend classes at the university there.

While in Glasgow, Alexander made friends with Greville Ewing and others who had broken from the Church of Scotland and formed independent churches. Ewing was associated with two brothers, James and Robert Haldane, who in turn were influenced by the thought of John Glas and Robert Sandeman. Glas, Sandeman, the Haldanes, and Ewing all wished to return to the practices of the New Testament church. Though they did not agree on every detail, these practices included local church leadership by elders, weekly Lord's Supper, Love Feasts with footwashing and the

Alexander Campbell

38

holy kiss, believer's baptism by immersion, opposition to ministerial titles such as "Reverend," and separation of church and state.

Alexander never joined any of these independent churches during his stay in Glasgow, yet he became increasingly dissatisfied with what he perceived as the narrowness of the Seceder Presbyterians. One of his last acts in Scotland before the family finally sailed successfully to America was to refuse quietly to commune with the Seceder church.

FATHER AND SON REUNION
After landing in New York, the family reunited in Western Pennsylvania in October 1809. Thomas and Alexander told of their separate difficulties with the Seceder Presbyterian Church. Alexander read a proof copy of the *Declaration and Address* and pledged to devote his life to promoting the principles he found there. Alexander began to study for the ministry under his father, and when the Brush Run church began in 1811, both father and son shared the preaching.

Also in 1811, Alexander married Margaret Brown, the daughter of a farmer who lived just over the line in what now is West Virginia. They lived on her father's farm until he eventually deeded the property to them. This property in what became Bethany, West Virginia, was to be the home of Alexander Campbell and the center of the movement he led until his death.

A year after their marriage, Margaret and Alexander had their first child, Jane, and her birth was more than a time of joy for the family; it also provoked a theological crisis. Alexander Campbell faced a decision: Should he baptize his infant daughter? And if not, should he himself be baptized as an adult? After months of study, he concluded that biblical baptism was immersion of believers, not sprinkling of infants. In June 1812, Matthias Luce, a Baptist minister, baptized Alexander and Thomas Campbell along with their wives and three others from the Brush Run Church.

Soon most of the members at Brush Run were immersed as believers. This further separated the Campbells from their Presbyterian roots since Presbyterians believed they should baptize infants. On the other hand, the practice of believer's immersion brought the Campbells into the orbit of the Baptists on the frontier. After much discussion, the Brush Run Church joined the Redstone Baptist Association in 1815.

BAPTISM AND SECTARIANISM

More than any other teaching, the early leaders' insistence on believer's immersion for forgiveness of sins set them apart from other Christian groups. Even Baptists, who practiced believer's immersion, did not emphasize its role in salvation.

Early in the history of the movement, some wondered if this emphasis on baptism would become divisive and sectarian. In 1830 Barton Stone worried that insisting on immersion could become a one-item sectarian creed that would exclude more Christians from union than any creed in existence. With some in the movement, this fear would become a reality. They would exclude all the unimmersed from the very name, "Christian."

In 1837, an unnamed woman from Lunenburg, Virginia, wrote Alexander Campbell expressing her surprise at his statement that he found Christians in all the Protestant groups. Campbell printed the letter in the *Millennial Harbinger* because it allowed him to answer several questions: Are only immersed believers entitled to the name Christian? Are all the Christians in the world in the movement Campbell led? Can we call the unimmersed "Christians" and still maintain that immersion is the biblical form of baptism?

Campbell was adamant in his reply to the letter: there must be Christians among the Protestant sects. Otherwise, he argued, there would have been no Christians in the world for centuries and Jesus' promise that the gates of hell would not prevail against the church (Matthew 16:18) would have proved false. Campbell said, "This cannot be; and therefore there are Christians among the sects."

The plea for unity, to "come out" of sectarianism, itself implies that there are Christians in the denominations. If all the Christians in the world were already united in the Stone-Campbell churches, then why would Campbell and others call Christians to come out of their sectarianism? In other words, to plead for unity necessarily means there are Christians to unify. Unfortunately, there were some even in Campbell's day who thought he wished to "make and lead a large exclusivist party" who claimed to be the only ones who were saved. He vehemently denied this, saying, "I think there are many, in most Protestant parties, whose errors and mistakes I hope the Lord will forgive."

Thus those in his day and our own who think they are the only Christians are out of step with the ideas that brought the movement into existence in the beginning. Some have tried to paint Alexander Campbell as inconsistent on this issue, claiming the "early Campbell" was a strict restorationist who saw his followers (or perhaps all the immersed) as the only Christians, while the "later Campbell" abandoned that position and became more ecumenical. Campbell himself refutes this charge by quoting his writings from the early years to show that he had always believed there are Christians among "the sects."

The belief that there are Christians other than those in our movement raises the question of baptism. As the Lunenburg letter asks, "What act of yours gave you the name of Christian?" In his preaching, his writing, and his debates, Campbell strongly defended believers' immersion as the biblical form of baptism and called on those baptized as infants to be immersed as adults. This emphasis led some of his followers to assume that only the immersed were Christians. They were shocked to find Campbell calling at least some of the un-immersed "Christians," and they accused him of abandoning his position on the importance of biblical baptism.

He replied by accusing some of his correspondents of being "ultraists," that is, legalists, on the subject of baptism. They had made baptism itself a savior, claiming it was the single standard by which one is judged to be a Christian. Campbell stated that he never taught such "water salvation." He refused to make even immersion the single standard of Christian faith and character. If forced to choose between one baptized as an infant and one immersed as a believer, he insisted that he would prefer the one who loved Christ most, saying, "Did I act otherwise, I would be a pure sectarian, a Pharisee among Christians."

41

Although baptism is central, Campbell wrote, it is not more important than Christian character. To deny the name Christian to those who display the character of Christ is to be the worst kind of sectarian. It is to promote the legalistic, exclusivist barriers that Campbell worked all his life to tear down.

Campbell strongly denied that admitting there may be Christians among the sects detracts from the importance of baptism. He saw himself steering a middle course between essentialists and non-essentialists on baptism. He claimed he did not detract from the authority of baptism simply by admitting the possibility of one being saved without it. However, Campbell taught that obedience to Christ and his ordinances (including baptism) were under usual conditions essential to salvation. One who willfully disdains or neglects baptism, he asserted, cannot be saved.

REFORMERS AMONG THE BAPTISTS

Joining the Redstone Baptist Association might look like an abandonment of the Campbells' goal to unite all Christians. How could they call for Christian unity when they belonged to a particular denomination? The Campbells, however, especially Thomas, did not see things that way. Instead, he felt that any visible unity was a step toward the ultimate unity of Christians. It was better to be part of a Baptist Association than to be a radically separatist individual congregation.

For the next fifteen years, the Campbells were reformers among the Baptists. Soon their supporters could be found in many Baptist congregations in addition to the Brush Run Church. Alexander Campbell became influential through his work as an educator, publisher and debater. At first, the Campbells had opposed debates as antithetical to Christian unity, but religious and political debating was a common practice in early America. After the Baptists approached him several times to defend believer's immersion in debate, Alexander finally agreed. In 1820, he faced John Walker and in 1823, William Maccalla, each Presbyterian ministers who argued for infant baptism. These debates, especially in their printed forms, were widely influential and convinced even Thomas

Campbell that debating could be a positive way to advance the cause of restoration and unity.

Although his debates made him the champion of believer's immersion, other teachings made Alexander suspect among many of the Baptists. As early as 1816, he offended many Baptists with his "Sermon on the Law" delivered at the meeting of the Redstone Association. In the sermon, Campbell made a sharp distinction between the Old and New Testaments, arguing that the Law of Moses was not authoritative for determining the beliefs and actions of the church.   Strong opposition from ministers in the Redstone Association led Campbell to transfer his membership to a congregation in the Mahoning Baptist Association, a group more favorable to Campbell's reforms. The churches of the Mahoning Association grew significantly due to the evangelism of Walter Scott (1796–1861). Jealousy of that growth and the increasing realization that the Campbells did not accept Baptist beliefs concerning such things as the meaning of baptism and the role of the minister soon caused several Baptist Associations to turn against them and any Baptist church that supported Campbell. Eventually, the Mahoning Association dissolved in 1830, and numerous Baptist Associations throughout Virginia, Ohio, and adjacent states also dissolved or divided, following the lead of the Campbells.

DISCIPLES OF CHRIST

Now an independent Movement, the churches led by Campbell faced the question of what to call themselves. Many individual followers preferred the name "Christian." Congregations often used a geographical or community name like "the Brush Run Church" or the "Wellsburg Church." Sometimes a sign on the outside of the building simply read, "Church of Christ" or "Christian Church."

This use of such generic names was in many ways intentional. They did not want an exclusive sectarian or denominational name. They wanted to call all followers of Jesus to unity. Nevertheless, one name increasingly characterized this congregationally organized church—Disciples of Christ. Alexander Campbell particularly preferred this name to "Christian." After all, the followers of

Jesus were called Disciples before they were called Christians. He also was nervous about having his movement confused with the Christian movements of New England and Virginia or even the one led by Barton Stone.

Yet, the similarities between these Disciples and the Stone Christians were so obvious that the two groups would eventually unite, though without the strong support of Alexander Campbell. The next chapter tells that part of the story.

QUESTIONS FOR DISCUSSION

1. Briefly describe Thomas Campbell's plan for producing Christian unity. What parts of that plan seem most and least workable? What parts could we profitably appropriate today?

2. Would it have been better if Thomas Campbell had not started a church but had continued to work in an inter-denominational Bible study? Can one be a Christian without belonging to a local church?

3. How did the church leaders he met in Scotland affect the ideas Alexander Campbell later had about the church?

4. What are the ways Alexander Campbell spread his ideas among the Baptists?

5. What did the early leaders mean when they said, "Christians only, not the only Christians?" Does accepting others as Christians mean we must abandon an emphasis on believer's immersion for forgiveness of sins?

6. Why did the Campbells eventually leave the Baptist Associations?

FOR FURTHER READING

Foster, Douglas A., Newell Williams, Paul M. Blowers, and Anthony L. Dunnavant, eds. *The Encyclopedia of the Stone-Campbell Movement*. Grand Rapids, Michigan: Eerdmans, 2004. See articles on Campbell, Alexander; Campbell, Thomas; Lunenburg Letter.

Williams, Newell, Douglas Foster, and Paul Blowers. *The Stone-Campbell Movement: A Global History*. St. Louis, Missouri: Chalice 2013. See pages 16–25.

Conkin, Paul K. *American Originals*. Chapel Hill: University of North Carolina Press, 1997. See pages 14–22.

Garrett, Leroy. *The Stone-Campbell Movement*. Joplin, Missouri: College Press, 1994. See pages 97–141.

Hughes, Richard T. *The Churches of Christ*. Westport, Connecticut: Praeger Press, 2001. See pages 3–98.

Olbricht, Thomas H. and Rollmann, Hans. *The Quest for Christian Unity, Peace, and Purity in Thomas Campbell's Declaration and Address*. Lanham, Maryland: Scarecrow Press, 2000.

The Stone and Campbell Movements Unite

A lexander Campbell first visited Kentucky in 1823, and the next year he met Stone in the living room of Stone's Georgetown home. The two sensed a close kinship of ideas and goals and expressed great respect for one another. Later in life, Stone said there were fewer faults in Campbell than in any man he knew, acknowledging that Campbell was the greatest promoter of the religious reformation in which they both were involved. In Stone's obituary notice in the 1844 *Millennial Harbinger,* Campbell hailed Stone as the instrument of bringing many out of human tradition to accept the Bible as their confession of faith and rule of life.

EARLY MOVES TOWARD UNION AND DIFFICULTIES

As early as the 1820s, members of the two bodies led by Stone and Campbell began asking why they weren't one. In August 1831, Stone replied to the question in his paper the *Christian Messenger.* As far as he and his movement were concerned, Stone stated, there was no reason they should not visibly unite since they were already one in spirit. Any reluctance to unite was on the part of the Reformers–the Campbell people–not from those on his side. He saw two reasons for their hesitance. First, the Stone movement allowed unimmersed people to be members of their churches and to take communion. Stone churches taught that people were to believe, repent, and be immersed for the forgiveness of sins. But they could not make immersion as crucial to Christianity as the Campbell Movement had. They taught the truth about the

47

importance and necessity of immersion, but exercised patience with those who were not convinced.

The second thing keeping them apart was the name each group had chosen. Like the Smith-Jones and O'Kelly churches, the Stone movement had always simply used the name Christian. Campbell preferred the label Disciples, which Stone admitted was a good scriptural name. But the Campbell churches used it, Stone asserted, to make sure no one confused them with the groups called Christian. It was a party name, just like Presbyterian or Baptist, because it distinguished those churches from other bodies of believers. Campbell responded with a sharp rebuke, claiming no one was asking them to give up the scriptural name Christian.

These articles and others that followed mirrored the deep differences between the two men and their Movements. Let's take a little more organized look at just how different they were. First, Barton Stone was opposed to traditional understandings of the Trinity. He did not see the doctrine taught in the New Testament as it was expressed in the creeds and confessions, especially the Westminster Confession. Growing from his rejection of the Trinity was his view of Jesus. He was willing to accept every biblical statement about Christ at face value without question. But for him that meant accepting that Christ was not equal to the Father. He was Son of God and Savior; the Father exalted him to a place above all others and seated him at his right hand; but he was not equal to the Father. The equality of Father and Son simply didn't make sense to Stone.

Campbell, on the other hand, was traditional in his views of the godhead and the nature of Christ. While he agreed that the word "Trinity" was not in the Bible, he believed that an understanding of the community within God—one deity yet three persons—was essential to the Christian faith. To demote Christ from full divinity was to question the very center of Christian belief, that Jesus is able to save us!

Despite his strong rejection of Calvinist predestination, Stone held a rather pessimistic view of human nature. Humans were capable of understanding and responding appropriately to the gospel message. Yet he saw a wide role for the Holy Spirit as necessary in convicting and converting sinners. Furthermore, human society as a whole, he insisted, was on a downhill slide that only the Second Coming of Christ would stop.

Campbell saw things differently. He was full of optimism about what humans could do by using their heads and working hard. America was the place prepared by God for the restoration of the church–the ancient gospel and order of things. After this restoration, all true Christians would come together, convert the world, and bring in the thousand-year reign of peace and prosperity on earth.

Stone and Campbell differed on their approach to evangelism. Stone had been a proponent of the revivals since his own experience at Cane Ridge. Here the Holy Spirit worked on the hearts of people to convict and convert them. Campbell hated the revivals and what he regarded as their raucous approach to conversion. Calm, clear, rational teaching of the gospel spelled out in the New Testament was the right way to convey truth and convince people to respond. The Holy Spirit worked through and along with the written word, never separately from it, to convince and convert sinners to Jesus.

Baptism was a point of difference as well. Campbell believed there were those who enjoyed the benefits of Christ's pardon and salvation who had never been immersed because of innocent misunderstanding. He did teach, however, that in order to be part of the reform–to be a member in one of the churches in his movement–a person must be immersed because that was the clear teaching of Scripture. As mentioned already, while Stone and his followers taught immersion, they practiced "open membership," allowing non-immersed believers to be members of their congregations and to participate fully in the life of their churches.

The Stone churches celebrated the Lord's Supper infrequently while the Campbell churches celebrated it every week. The Stone churches had a much more developed sense of the need to organize the ministry. Like the Presbyterians, they distinguished between elders who were ordained ministers and those who were not officially ordained. The Campbell churches were extremely anti-clergy and much more democratic in their attitudes about who could do what in the church.

These were not minor differences! They reflected contradictory understandings of the nature of God, humankind, salvation, the church, and the end of time. How could two movements as dissimilar as these even consider uniting? It is hard to imagine, but thousands in both were convinced that the things they held in common far outweighed their differences. They agreed on the rejection of human creeds and confessions of faith as tests of fellowship. They rejected loyalty to denominational bodies that separated them from other believers. All had a commitment to God and to his written word as the only source of authority on religion. All wanted the visible unity of Christ's church.

There were some practical matters that made union a difficult undertaking. There were no general officers or central offices to make decisions and pronounce that a union had taken place between the two groups. The only governing authority in either movement was the leadership in each local congregation. There were no edicts from on high–the union had to happen among the churches in each city, town or village throughout the country.

THE UNION TAKES SHAPE

Barton Stone, then living in Georgetown, had become a close friend of John T. Johnson (1788–1856), a former Baptist preacher who now followed Alexander Campbell's reform ideas. They had persuaded the two congregations in Georgetown to unite in October 1831, and others proposed travel through Kentucky to unite other groups of Christians and Reformers. First, however, the leaders decided to hold two four-day conferences—at Georgetown over Christmas weekend and at the Hill Street church in Lexington over New Year's weekend. At Lexington several leaders from the two groups spoke, including one of the most widely known leaders of the Campbell Movement in Kentucky, Racoon John Smith (1784–1868). Smith and Stone were the final speakers at the concluding session Saturday afternoon. Smith spoke of the fact that God has

John Smith   John Rogers

only one people on earth and that the Bible, the one book God had given Christians, exhorts them to be one family. He openly admitted that there were serious differences between the two movements, mentioning the issues of God's nature, the Trinity, and the atonement. These have been topics of discussion for centuries, he explained, and are as far from settled now as they ever have been. The precise positions that Christians might take on these or other issues are not part of the gospel. No heaven was promised to those who hold one position or the other, and no hell was threatened to those who deny them.

Then Smith made one of the most famous statements in Stone-Campbell history: "Let us then, my brethren, be no longer Campbellites or Stoneites, New Lights or Old Lights, or any other kind of lights. But let us come to the Bible and the Bible alone, as the only book in creation that can give us all the Light we need."

Stone spoke next and concluded that he had no objection to the basis of union Smith had laid down. He then turned and gave Smith his hand in fellowship, symbolizing the unity that was becoming a reality. The next day, a Sunday, January 1, 1832, the two congregations met together and took the Lord's Supper as one body. This service seemed to seal the union.

Stone was elated. In his report of the meeting in the *Christian Messenger*, he described the spirit of union as spreading like fire in dry stubble. He explained that the elders and people had commissioned John Smith and John Rogers (1800–1867), formerly of the Campbell and Stone Movements respectively, to travel among the churches to tell them what had happened in Lexington in order to "increase and consolidate the union." Smith and Rogers spent three years doing just that. Campbell took notice of the meeting in the March issue of his *Millennial Harbinger*, concluding that if the groups present really had renounced their speculations, there was nothing to do but bid them Godspeed.

REAL UNITY AND GROWTH

Even with all the problems involved, the story of the union of the Stone and Campbell movements is phenomenal. How was it possible for two groups that were so different from each other to even consider coming together? It happened because the people involved believed union was God's will and that they shared what was most important in Christianity–one body, one Spirit, one Lord, one faith, one baptism, one God and Father of all. Most of all, they loved one another as fellow children of God with all their imperfections.

When Stone and Campbell churches began to unite in the early 1830s, they together numbered around twenty-five thousand members, mainly in Kentucky and Ohio. By 1861, the united movement numbered almost two hundred thousand in twenty-nine states and two territories. It was during this period that the Disciples of Christ (as they were generally known) became a nationwide church, by some estimates the fourth largest religious group in the country.

WALTER SCOTT AND THE NEW EVANGELISM

This phenomenal growth largely resulted from the influence of one man, Walter Scott (1796–1861). Born in Scotland, Scott grew up in the Church of Scotland and received his education at the University of Edinburgh. In 1818, he came to America, eventually settling near Pittsburgh. There he taught school and worshipped with a Scottish Baptist church.

In 1821, Scott met Alexander Campbell, and they soon became friends. Scott contributed articles on evangelism to the initial issue of Campbell's *Christian Baptist* (Scott was the one who suggested the name for the journal). In 1827, the Mahoning Baptist Association appointed Scott as their evangelist. The year before, the seventeen churches in the Association had a total of thirty-four baptisms. In his first year as evangelist, Scott had nearly a thousand baptisms, doubling the size of most of the churches. Indeed, Scott averaged a thousand baptisms per year for the next thirty years of his life.

What made him so successful was a new method of evangelism. Although the churches of the Campbell movement had been in existence for several years and all practiced believer's immersion, they had not found a simple answer to the question, "What must I do to be saved?" In his study of Scripture, Scott found that answer which he called "the ancient gospel" or (in the words of one of his later book titles) *The Gospel Restored*.

Scott originally summarized that gospel under six points. Humans should do three things to be saved: believe, repent, and be baptized. God makes three promises to those who do these things: forgiveness of sins, the gift of the Holy Spirit, and eternal life. Eventually, Scott reduced the six to an easily remembered "five-finger exercise"—faith, repentance, baptism, forgiveness of sins, and the gift of the Holy Spirit.

Such a formula could become legalistic. What kept Scott from using it in a legalistic way was his constant emphasis on the central teaching of Christianity, that Jesus is the Christ. Scott called this "the golden oracle," later writing a massive volume entitled *The Messiahship, or Great Demonstration, Written for the Union of Christians, on Christian Principles, as Plead for in the Current Reformation*. This lengthy title shows that Scott's view of restoration was

Walter Scott

53

directly in line with that of Stone and the Campbells. Restoration centered on Christ for the purpose of uniting all Christians.

Although Scott began his preaching of the restored gospel before the union with the Stone movement in 1832, evangelists in the united movement copied his method, accounting for much of the growth of the Disciples through the nineteenth century. This is why many consider him one of the four founders of the movement along with Barton Stone, Thomas Campbell, and Alexander Campbell.

SCHOOLS, PAPERS, AND MISSIONS

Many of the early leaders, including Thomas and Alexander Campbell, saw themselves foremost as teachers. It is not surprising, then, that the Stone-Campbell Movement, along with every major religious group in nineteenth century America, began colleges and schools. The first college in the movement was Bacon College, Georgetown, Kentucky, founded in 1836 primarily as an engineering school. Walter Scott served briefly as its first President. In 1839, Bacon College moved to Harrodsburg, Kentucky, was rechartered in 1858 as Kentucky University, and later merged with other schools to become Transylvania University in Lexington.

In 1841, Alexander Campbell founded Bethany College near his home in Bethany, West Virginia. Bethany College is still in its original location and still associated with Disciples of Christ.

Bethany College

Franklin College near Nashville, Tennessee, began in 1845. Tolbert Fanning (1810–1874), the founder of the school, did not believe in endowments for colleges. That partially explains the short life of Franklin College. Closed by the Civil War in 1861, it reopened briefly in 1865, but soon closed permanently as the result of a campus fire.

From 1840–1866, Disciples began thirty-two colleges including (with their founding dates) Burritt College, Spencer, Tennessee (1848); Hiram College, Hiram, Ohio (1850); Butler University, Indianapolis, Indiana (1854); Culver-Stockton College, Canton, Missouri (1853); and Eureka College, Eureka, Illinois (1855).

Although not intended primarily for ministerial training, the colleges served that function. Many of the significant church leaders in the nineteenth century were products of the colleges, particularly Bethany. In a congregationally organized movement, the colleges provided one means of fellowship and unity of thought among the churches.

Religious papers also provided unity (and sometimes disunity) to the Movement, serving as the forum to discuss ideas and issues. An old truism is that the Disciples did not have bishops, they had editors, editors who sometimes ruled with an iron fist.

Alexander Campbell's influence grew primarily through his monthly periodicals, first the *Christian Baptist* (1823–1830), then the *Millennial Harbinger* (1830–1866). Other leaders greatly extended their influence through journals. Barton Stone edited the *Christian Messenger* from 1826–1844. Walter Scott had the aptly named *Evangelist* (1832–1844). In 1855, Tolbert Fanning founded the influential *Gospel Advocate*. The *American Christian Review*, edited from 1858 by Benjamin Franklin (1812–1878), eventually became the most widely read paper in the movement before the American Civil War.

In addition, there were dozens of short-lived papers with limited circulation (including one named the *Heretic Detector*). These papers did detect heresy, debate issues, promote unity, and suggest programs. More than any other factor, the journals formed the web that held the Stone-Campbell Movement together.

From 1845–1848, Alexander Campbell penned a series of articles in the *Millennial Harbinger* on church cooperation, eventually calling for church-wide cooperation to promote Bible distribution, benevolence, and missions. As early as 1829, church leaders in local areas had met to share information and encouragement. By 1844, regular statewide meetings were being held in Kentucky, Ohio, Indiana, and Tennessee. The first organizations formed in response to the call for church-wide support among the Disciples were the American Christian Bible Society, begun in 1845, and the Sunday School and Tract Society, begun in 1846. David S. Burnet (1808–1867) led both organizations and also took the initiative in beginning the Missionary Society.

Campbell's call for a general convention of the Disciples finally happened in Cincinnati in October 1849. The hope was for each congregation to send delegates to the convention, but many congregations did not participate and several individuals simply came on their own. The convention was therefore more of a mass meeting of 151 "messengers" from about 100 churches than a representative body. Those present organized the American Christian Missionary Society and chose Alexander Campbell its first President (though Campbell was not present due to illness).

As we will see, the right of the Missionary Society to exist eventually became a divisive issue among Disciples, contributing to the split between Disciples of Christ and Churches of Christ. What concerns us here is the Society's role in sending the first Disciple missionaries from America to other countries.

Since Jerusalem was where Peter first preached the gospel in the Book of Acts, it seemed fitting that the first missionary supported by the Society should take the restored gospel there. They chose James T. Barclay (1807–1874), a well-educated physician, for the task. Barclay and his family had two tours of duty in Jerusalem, 1850–1854 and 1858–1861. They went knowing nothing of the languages spoken there and little of the culture. They made a few converts and left no lasting church.

Some in the North criticized the American Christian Missionary Society for sending Barclay because he was a slave owner. Though many southern Disciples held slaves, in 1853 the Society bought the freedom of a Kentucky-born slave, Alexander Cross, and sent him as a missionary to freed slaves in Liberia. Cross arrived in Liberia in January 1854, but died of fever two months after his arrival.

The only early mission that had even modest success was that of the third missionary sent by the Society, J. O. Beardslee (1814–1879), who worked in Jamaica from 1858–1866. But false allegations even clouded his work.

Since these were the only missionaries sent by the Society before the American Civil War, one is tempted to call its efforts a failure. Yet, what may be most significant about the Society is not what it accomplished in missions but what it said about the developing identity of the Disciples. From two small fellowships in 1832, the church had grown through evangelism, education, and publications to be a substantial religious body, capable of organizing for international action.

QUESTIONS FOR DISCUSSION

1. How important is it for local congregations to agree internally on doctrinal issues?

2. What do you think was the most serious doctrinal difference between the Stone and Campbell movements at the time of the union? Why do you believe that one is the most serious?

3. Would it be possible today for local congregations to experience a union like those that occurred in the 1830s and following? If so, how? If not, why?

4. What was Walter Scott's greatest contribution to the churches of the Stone-Campbell Movement?

5. What were the six points Scott used to summarize the gospel? Is this a fair summary? What did he omit or what should he have omitted?

6. Who were the first three international missionaries of the Stone-Campbell Movement? Where were they sent? How were they supported? What does this say about the Movement in the late 1800s?

7. Are there ways that the churches of the Stone-Campbell Movement can act together as a whole today?

For Further Reading

Foster, Douglas A., Newell Williams, Paul M. Blowers, and Anthony L. Dunnavant, eds. *The Encyclopedia of the Stone-Campbell Movement*. Grand Rapids, Michigan: Eerdmans, 2004. See articles on Higher Education; Views of in the Movement; Scott, Walter.

Williams, Newell, Douglas Foster, and Paul Blowers. *The Stone-Campbell Movement: A Global History*. St. Louis, Missouri: Chalice 2013. See pages 25–34.

Carisse Berryhill. "From Facts to Feeling: The Rhetoric of Moral Formation in Alexander Campbell's Morning Lectures at Bethany College," in *And the Word Became Flesh: Studies in History, Communication, and Scripture in Memory of Michael W. Casey*. Edited by Thomas H. Olbricht and David Fleer. Eugene, OR: Pickwick, 2009.

Garrett, Leroy. *The Stone-Campbell Movement: The Story of the American Restoration Movement*. Joplin, Missouri: College Press, 1994. See pages 143–196.

Toulouse, Mark G., ed. *Walter Scott: A Nineteenth Century Evangelical*. Saint Louis: Chalice Press, 1999.

The Great Divide of the Civil War

Perhaps the saddest story of the Stone-Campbell Movement is how these Christians in America so dedicated to unity divided over the issues of race, slavery, and sectionalism.

SLAVERY, RACE, AND THE CHURCHES

In 1860, there were about 1200 congregations in the north and about 800 in the south. Many were in border states like Kentucky, Ohio and Missouri where differences over the issues that led to war were especially strong. Though many difficult political and social issues fueled the conflict, at its heart it was about slavery and race. Members of the churches of the Stone-Campbell Movement were just as much a part of the heated discussions as anyone. Their attitudes about blacks and slavery reflected the same spectrum as the rest of America.

Both Barton Stone and Alexander Campbell opposed slavery though both owned slaves at different times in their lives. Stone freed all his slaves by 1804, and in 1834 moved to Illinois to free others inherited from his wife's mother since Kentucky law forbade such. Stone was a supporter of the American Colonization Society for several years. This group planned to end slavery over time by buying slaves from masters and sending them "back" to the west African nation of Liberia, purchased and established by the society for that purpose. Frustration with the Colonization effort eventually led Stone to support abolition—the immediate freeing of all slaves by law.

Campbell detailed his position on slavery in 1845 in a series of eight articles published in the *Millennial Harbinger* entitled "Our Position to American Slavery." The Methodist and Baptist Churches had just divided over slavery, and the debate over the annexation of Texas to the Union as a slave state threatened a major crisis in the nation and the movement.

He spent much energy explaining why the issue of slavery must not divide the churches. Though opposed to the institution, he appeared to be defending its existence in most of the articles! Nowhere in the Scriptures, he claimed, is the relation of master to slave sinful and immoral in itself. On the contrary, the Scriptures seek to regulate the relationship, not abolish it. When he finally began to explain why he opposed slavery, it was because it was not in keeping with the "genius of the age." He supported a gradual approach as the best way to end slavery without causing disruption to the nation and its institutions.

Campbell was not primarily interested in the welfare of the enslaved people. He was interested in the unity of his reform movement and regarded the conflict over slavery as a great threat. He concluded his series with the assertion that "no Christian community, governed by the Bible, can constitutionally and rightfully make the simple relation of master and slave a term of Christian fellowship or a subject of discipline."

Pardee Butler

Pardee Butler (1816–1888) was perhaps the most outspoken abolitionist in the Stone-Campbell Movement. When he moved to Kansas in 1855 to work as an evangelist, his message focused on abolitionism as the gospel's response to the evil of slavery. When the American Christian Missionary Society (ACMS) refused to support Butler unless he stopped preaching his anti-slavery views, a group of abolitionist church members from

Ohio and Indiana formed a rival missionary society in 1859 that provided funds for Butler's work until it rejoined the ACMS in 1863.

Without question, the strongest pro-slavery voice in the Stone-Campbell Movement was James Shannon (1799–1859). He asserted what many whites took for granted, that blacks were inferior and not capable of living responsibly as free people. Nature, the United States Constitution, and the Bible all clearly approved slavery, he said, and any attempt to violate the rights of masters to hold slaves as legal property should be resisted even to the point of war.

In fact, Disciples in the South held many slaves, some of them fellow church members. African Americans were members at Cane Ridge and Brush Run from the beginning of the movement. Evangelism of African-Americans was important as shown by black evangelists Samuel Buckner and Alexander Campbell who were ordained and planted churches in Kentucky and North Carolina. Although members at predominately white congregations, African Americans were forced to sit in the balcony or the rear of the auditorium and to take communion after whites. By the 1830s there were some separate black congregations with their own ministers.

THE CHURCHES IN THE CIVIL WAR

Just as with later divisive issues the question of slavery and slaveholders was a matter each congregation had to work out for itself. We didn't have a national organization that could facilitate the kind of division seen among the Baptists, Methodists, and Presbyterians. Or did we?

Though by no means working like a Presbyterian General Assembly or Methodist Conference, the Stone-Campbell Movement did have a national organization—the American Christian Missionary Society. Headquartered in the north, in Cincinnati, Ohio, the annual meetings had always enjoyed attendance from across the country. When the war began, however, southerners were no longer able to come to meetings.

61

David Lipscomb

Just as many leaders in the movement had been "moderates" on the issue of slavery, many (led again by Campbell himself) refused to endorse either side in the war. It is not surprising, then, that outsiders began to question the loyalty to the Union of the American Christian Missionary Society and the churches it represented. At the October 1861 meeting, some members introduced a resolution calling on the churches of the movement to do everything in their power to support the Union.

When word got back to southern church leaders what had happened, the reaction was swift. Tolbert Fanning in Nashville, Tennessee, had been urging southern Christians to stay out of the conflict. When he heard about the resolution, he took it to mean that the ACMS was encouraging its supporters to join the Union armies and participate in the murder of the Southern people. Unless those who had passed this resolution repented of what they had done, Fanning was clear that he could not regard them as fellow Christians. Though many church leaders in the north like Benjamin Franklin (1812–1878) had remained neutral through the war, the society had chosen sides in a political and military conflict. The man who would become the foremost church leader in the south after the Civil War, David Lipscomb (1831–1917), wrote in 1866 that the Society had committed a great wrong against the church and the cause of God. Unless there is repentance of the wrong, he asserted, "It should not receive the confidence of the Christian brotherhood."

WERE WE DIVIDED BY THE CIVIL WAR?

The notion that anyone in America before, during, and after the Civil War could have remained unaffected by such a momentous event is remarkably naive. The war created two different moods in the country–one in the North and one in the South–that no one could escape. Northerners had won the war. There was a general sense of victory, progress, and prosperity, mixed with a desire to punish or rehabilitate the south. Southerners had been defeated. To survive, they interpreted their defeat as discipline from God to keep them from becoming like the materialistic north and to preserve their virtues as an example of God's ideal culture.

Thus, it was not just the war but its aftermath, particularly Reconstruction in the South, that contributed to the breaking of Christian fellowship. After the war, many churches in the prosperous northern cities became successful in society. They built large buildings with expensive stained glass. They preferred educated ministers. They could even afford expensive organs for their new buildings. As we shall see, some opposed instrumental music in worship more for its "worldliness" than because they thought it "unscriptural." The Disciples in the North became so accepted in the culture that one of their number, James A. Garfield (1831–1881), became President of the United States.

By contrast, Southern members after the war faced starvation, disease, and economic ruin. Although some Northern church leaders made the effort to raise humanitarian support for the South, little aid arrived. To Southerners, it was inconceivable that their fellow Christians in the North could spend money on buildings and organs while their brothers and sisters in the South were struggling just to stay alive.

The North-South division was real and substantial. In the data collected by the 1906 U.S. Census of Religious Bodies, two-thirds of the Disciples of Christ would be in the North and two-thirds of the Churches of Christ in the South. That is too much of a coincidence for anyone to deny that the war divided us, though it is more complex than simple sectionalism. Clearly the war and its consequences shaped the discussion of the religious issues in the division—the Missionary Society and instrumental music—as well as the approaches to biblical interpretation that stood behind those religious issues.

OPPOSITION TO THE MISSIONARY SOCIETY

When the American Christian Missionary Society formed in Cincinnati in 1849, it encountered little opposition from preachers and editors in the church. Two of those who were later most vehement in their opposition—Tolbert Fanning and Benjamin Franklin—had even once served as officers of the Society.

Fanning was the first to break with the Society. When he began the *Gospel Advocate* in 1855, one purpose of the journal was to give the "Society issue" a thorough discussion. By 1857, Fanning was convinced that the Society was not authorized by Scripture. Yet he refused at this point to break fellowship with those who supported the Society. He even addressed the Society's annual meeting in 1859 rejoicing that the movement was still united. It was only after the Society's pro-Union resolutions in 1861 and 1863 that Fanning began to make the Society a matter of fellowship.

The same pattern holds with Benjamin Franklin, who edited the popular religious paper the *American Christian Review* published in Cincinnati, the headquarters of the Society. Franklin served as a secretary for the Society for thirteen years, but in 1866 turned completely against it. Although from the North, he also was scandalized by the Society's abandonment of neutrality and pacifism during the war.

The arguments against the Society were generally consistent among those who opposed it. It had become involved in sectional politics. It was an inefficient way to do mission work. It dictated to the churches. The most telling argument was the silence of the Bible on church organization beyond the local congregation. Those who supported the Society took that silence as permission. Those who opposed it believed silence prohibited the formation of a missionary society. Eventually most preachers and papers in the North, including the influential *Christian Standard*, supported the Missionary Society and other organizations for benevolent and mission work. Those in the South generally opposed any organization beyond the local congregation.

INSTRUMENTAL MUSIC IN WORSHIP

Discussion of the propriety of using instrumental music in worship was not unique to the Stone-Campbell Movement. Zwingli and Calvin had opposed the practice during the Reformation. In America, Congregational churches did not use instruments in worship until after the Revolutionary War. Baptists and Presbyterians battled over its propriety in the nineteenth century. The matter was not an issue in the early history of the movement, perhaps because few frontier churches could afford instruments. The first recorded instance of an instrument used in worship among the Stone-Campbell churches was in Midway, Kentucky, in 1859. The minister, L. L. Pinkerton (1812–1875), brought in a melodeon to help singing that was so bad it "scared even the rats from worship."

Only after the American Civil War did many churches bring in instruments. Those who did argued that they were aids to singing and appealed to a new generation of worshippers. Opposition to instruments came largely from the South and from the rural North, though not exclusively. Part of that opposition was social and economic: how could northern churches squander money on organs while many of their southern brothers and sisters were destitute? Others argued that the use of instruments put too much emphasis on the beauty and sophistication of the music to the neglect of glorifying God. Their use did not promote simple spiritual worship.

As with the Missionary Society, the primary objection to instrumental music in worship came from the silence of Scripture. Since the New Testament mentioned singing but not instruments in worship, instruments were prohibited. On the other hand, those who supported their use argued that silence permitted instruments as an aid to singing just as silence permitted songbooks, song leaders, and church buildings as aids to worship. Interestingly, some applied the argument from silence differently to the issues. Thus, prominent leaders such as J. W. McGarvey (1829–1911) and Moses Lard supported the Missionary Society, but opposed instruments in worship.

Why was the instrumental music issue so divisive? Perhaps because it was so visible. One could worship for years with a congregation and not know which members disagreed with your position on Missionary Societies and other issues. One could see immediately on entering a church building whether or not that congregation used instrumental music.

Although many leaders tried for a while to avoid making the instrument a matter of fellowship, it soon became one. After all, what could those conscientiously opposed to instruments do when one was introduced into their congregation? It seemed to most that they had no choice but to form a separate church.

Steps toward Division

There were other divisive issues discussed during this time such as the legitimacy of a salaried settled ministry and methods of raising funds outside of the Sunday contribution. In spite of the disagreement on these and on instrumental music and the Missionary Society, there was still something of an uneasy unity through the 1870s. By the 1880s, however, some were calling for recognition of a division they claimed had already occurred.

Chief among those was Daniel Sommer (1850–1940), who had followed Benjamin Franklin as editor of the *American Christian Review*. Sommer saw the changes among the churches during the previous thirty years as examples of apostasy. He made a distinction between "the Church of Christ" and the "so-called Christian Church." In 1889, Peter Warren, an elder at Sand Creek, Illinois, read Sommer's "An Address and Declaration" (apparently a play on Thomas Campbell's *Declaration and Address*) outlining his plan to save the Movement from "innovations and corruptions." If leaders and churches would not give up practices such as instrumental music, support of the Society, located preachers, and others, then Sommer said "we cannot and will not regard them as brethren."

Most leaders in both the North and the South were not as quick as Sommer to proclaim a division. Eventually, though, they had to admit it. For many years, David Lipscomb was extremely reluctant to acknowledge the division. By 1904, however, he was compiling a list of faithful churches and preachers, another way that a congregational movement identifies a split. In 1906, when asked by the Director of the United States religious census if he should list

Churches of Christ separately from Disciples of Christ, Lipscomb painfully agreed that they were now two distinct bodies.

UNITY OR DIVISION?

The story of this and subsequent divisions in the Stone-Campbell Movement is one of the most embarrassing parts of our heritage. How could a group that began as a unity movement later fracture and splinter? How could significant differences between the Stone and Campbell groups be overcome for the sake of unity in 1832, while seemingly less important issues divide us by 1906?

At least part of the answer to those questions lies in attitude. Certainly, doctrines must be maintained to be faithful to God. The New Testament is greatly concerned with doctrinal purity. But the doctrines at the heart of the gospel always center on Christ. The issues that usually divide us do not. How can that be? Because we make those issues more important and divisive than they should be.

Even in the decades following the Civil War some refused to split with their brothers and sisters over the issues and the ill feelings caused by the war. One such man was T. B. Larimore (1843–1929). Born in poverty in east Tennessee, Larimore was baptized in Kentucky in 1864 and later attended Franklin College near Nashville, studying under Tolbert Fanning. Larimore spent the rest of his life as an educator and travel-

ing evangelist, operating Mars Hill Academy near Florence, Alabama from 1871 to 1887.

Thus, Larimore was a loyal son of the South, influenced by some of the strongest opponents of the Missionary Society and instrumental music in worship. He personally never supported either practice. However, he refused to declare himself publicly on these issues because he believed the body of Christ should not divide over such matters.

T. B. Larimore

He saw his duty as a Christian evangelist to proclaim the good news of Christ. He had nothing to do with those questions over which "the wisest and best of men disagreed."

He was successful in his evangelistic work, baptizing over ten thousand people in his lifetime. But because of his visibility, he was under intense pressure to take sides on the issues. It exasperated many that he would not line up with either side. Partisans on both sides criticized him harshly, but he consistently refused to defend himself. The only way to avoid division, he thought, was to allow freedom in matters of opinion.

In this regard, Larimore reflected the heritage of Thomas Campbell and the *Declaration and Address*. When Campbell spoke of "being silent where the Bible is silent," he allowed for strong opinions on what that silence meant. Some might think silence permits; others might be sure it forbids. The "silence" Campbell called for was the refusal to make those opinions divisive matters of faith.

Many in Churches of Christ turned Campbell's teaching upside down, insisting that "being silent" meant prohibiting any practice not mentioned in the New Testament. They even went farther and refused fellowship to those who approved of those practices. This is what Larimore would not do. He would not break relations with those who were (in his opinion) wrong on "the issues."

Larimore's fellowship with Disciples of Christ and Churches of Christ was in deed, not just in word. He continued to preach wherever he was invited, and was on the List of Preachers in the Disciples Yearbook until 1925. If everyone in his day had imitated his attitude, the "issues" would never have divided the churches. In any age, it seems like a good idea to follow the Golden Rule, to think the best of fellow Christians, to pray more and dispute less. That is the legacy of Larimore.

QUESTIONS FOR DISCUSSION

1. Should Christians and churches become involved in the political and social issues of the day? Why or why not?

2. What do you see as the core issue for the churches of the Stone-Campbell Movement regarding slavery in the period before the Civil War? Could the division connected with the Civil War have been avoided?

3. How did post-Civil War conditions affect the discussion over the Missionary Society and instrumental music? Are there ever "pure" discussions of doctrinal issues or do circumstances always color our thinking?

4. What are some good arguments for a cappella music in worship? What are some bad arguments for it?

5. Can we fellowship others who disagree with us on these issues? On other issues? What would that fellowship look like?

6. Would following the Golden Rule eliminate our doctrinal differences with other Christians? Would it help our relations with them?

FOR FURTHER READING

Foster, Douglas A., Newell Williams, Paul M. Blowers, and Anthony L. Dunnavant, eds. *The Encyclopedia of the Stone-Campbell Movement.* Grand Rapids, Michigan: Eerdmans, 2004. See articles on Civil War, The; Instrumental Music; Larimore, Theophilus Brown; Missionary Societies, Controversy over; and Slavery, the Movement and.

Williams, Newell, Douglas Foster, and Paul Blowers. *The Stone-Campbell Movement: A Global* History. St. Louis, Missouri: Chalice 2013. See pages 35–84.

Foster, Douglas A. *Will the Cycle Be Unbroken? Churches of Christ Face the 21st Century* (Abilene: ACU Press, 1994). See pages 147–159.

Garrett, Leroy. *The Stone-Campbell Movement.* (Joplin, Missouri: College Press, 1994). See pages 333–355, 381–405.

Harrell, David Edwin, Jr. *Quest for a Christian America: The Disciples of Christ and American Society to 1866.* Nashville: Disciples of Christ Historical Society, 1966. See pages 91–138.

Maxey, Robert Tibbs. *Alexander Campbell and the Peculiar Institution.* El Paso, TX: Spanish American Evangelism, 1986.

Poyner, Barry C. *Bound to Slavery: James Shannon and the Restoration Movement.* Ft. Worth: Star Bible Publications, 1999.

The Christian Church (Disciples of Christ)

A s we saw in the last chapter, Disciples of Christ shared in the prosperity and optimism of the North after the Civil War. The increasing international stature of the United States, the growth of cities, the rise of the sciences and new ways of thinking greatly influenced Disciples. Many dreamed of taking the gospel to the entire world and of eradicating social evils of injustice and poverty.

DEVELOPING STRUCTURES FOR MISSION

As early as the 1840s, Alexander Campbell had called for a more effective means of cooperation among the churches, especially in light of the call to mission. That call resulted in the establishment of the American Christian Missionary Society in 1849 (later called the General Christian Missionary Convention). After the American Civil War, Disciples began to develop other structures for mission. Caroline Neville Pearre (1831–1910) formed the Christian Woman's Board of Mission in 1874. In 1886, Matilda Hart Younkin (1843–1908) began the National Benevolent Association to care for the sick and for orphans. These organizations gave a place for women to exercise ministry in the

Caroline Neville Pearre

church, leading to the ordination of Clara Hale Babcock (1850–1924) in 1889.

These and other organizations, society, and boards, led some in the church to call for a more central organization to avoid needless repetition of effort and competition for donations. The 1906 Convention in Buffalo, N.Y. suggested the church form a convention of representative delegates from congregations, similar to what Alexander Campbell had suggested. It would take decades for a similar plan to come to fruition, although in 1917, the Convention approved a new constitution and name, The International Convention (because it included Canada and the United States).

In the meantime, new boards developed. For example, growing out of a board in the American Christian Missionary Society, the Board of Education of Disciples of Christ was formed in 1914 primarily to raise and distribute funds for Disciple Colleges. The board eventually became Higher Education and Leadership Ministries, serving as a connection between the church and seventeen colleges and universities and more than 140 campus ministries.

In 1920, the American Christian Missionary Society, the Christian Woman's Board of Missions, the Foreign Christian Missionary Society, the Board of Church Extension, the National Benevolent Association, and the Board of Ministerial Relief were combined into the United Christian Missionary Society. This was a first step toward a long and thoughtful path to consolidation and centralization of resources.

However, Disciples in this period faced theological and social tensions connected to the church's structure. Some were disturbed about charges that the missionary societies supported open membership, accepting unimmersed believers into the churches. Some objected to the idea of delegate assemblies where voting on issues and structures took place. Some had concerns about theological liberalism in the context of the Fundamentalist-Liberal controversy. As a result, a non-voting annual meeting, the North American Christian Convention, was formed in 1927. Eventually these concerns would lead to a division. That story will be told more fully in the next chapter.

In an effort to clarify some of these issues, avoid division, and thoughtfully consider what structures were needed for the church, the International Convention in 1934 created the Commission on Restudy of the Disciples of Christ, which met three times yearly until 1949. Leaders on the Commission included F.D. Kershner (1875–1953), R.H. Miller (1874–1963), O.L. Shelton (1895–1959), C. C. Morrison (1874–1966), and Dean E. Walker (1898–1988). The members of the Commission reached consensus on many theological matters but were unable to prevent division. The Commission's work set the stage for the creation of the Panel of Scholars, a fifteen member commission that met twice yearly from 1957 through 1962. The Panel, which included Ralph G. Wilburn (1909–1986), Ronald E. Osborn (1917–1998), and William Barnett Blakemore (1912–1975), discussed Disciples theology and organization in light of contemporary scholarship, publishing its findings in 1963 as *The Renewal of the Church: The Panel Reports.*

The work of the Panel of Scholars led in 1961 to the Commission on Brotherhood Restructure, which presented a Provisional Design for the Christian Church (Disciples of Christ) to congregations, regions, and church agencies in 1966. After two years of study and response, the Provisional Design was accepted at the Kansas City Convention in 1968.

The result was a structure based on covenant that recognized three manifestations of church—congregational, regional, and general. The church's organization was intended to be biblical, comprehensive, interrelated, ecumenical, and faithful, expressing both unity and diversity. The various agencies or units of the general church had no formal jurisdictional authority over the congregations, but were designed to serve the church and aid in carrying out the body's mission commitments including reconciliation.

PRACTICING UNITY AND ECUMENISM

From the beginning, Christian unity has been at the very heart of the Stone-Campbell Movement's existence. In the last century many who worked for Christian unity chose the biblical term "ecumenical" to describe their work because they wanted a word that

Peter Ainslie

included unity and evangelism. That is why the World Council of Churches in 1951 defined *ecumenical* in the light of the original Greek, "to describe everything that relates to the whole task of the whole church to bring the Gospel to the whole world. It therefore covers . . . both unity and mission in the context of the whole world."

The modern ecumenical movement usually dates its beginning to the Edinburgh World Mission Conference of 1910. In that same year, Peter Ainslie (1867–1934) of the Disciples founded the Council on Christian Union to coordinate their ecumenical witness. Peter Ainslie, George Walker Buckner (1893–1988), George G. Beazley, Jr (1914–1973), Paul A. Crow, Jr (1931–), and Robert K. Welsh have led what is today called the Council on Christian Unity.

Disciples were founding members of the Federal Council of Churches in America (1908), the Canadian Council of Churches (1944), the World Council of Churches (1948), and the National Council of Churches of Christ in the U.S.A. (1950).

However, Disciples not only joined Federations of churches, but also pursued church union with several denominations through the Conference on Church Union from 1946–1958 and the Consultation on Church Union, begun in 1960 and resulting in 2002 in Churches Uniting in Christ, a covenant relationship among eleven Christian communions: the African Methodist Episcopal Church, the African Methodist Episcopal Zion Church, the Christian Church (Disciples of Christ), the Christian Methodist Episcopal Church, the Episcopal Church, the Evangelical Lutheran Church in America, the International Council of Community Churches, the Moravian Church (Northern Province), the Presbyterian Church (USA), the United Church of Christ, and the United Methodist Church.

Disciples have also been involved in international theological dialogues with Roman Catholics, the World Communion of Reformed Churches, the Evangelical Lutheran Church in Finland, and other churches through the Disciples Ecumenical Consultative Council. One significant dialogue in light of the story of disunion told in the previous chapter is the Stone-Campbell Dialogue begun in 1999, whose purpose is to develop relationships and trust within the three North American streams of the Stone-Campbell Movement through worship and through charitable and frank dialogue, "that the world may believe".

Their global ecumenical work also led Disciples into a new view of mission work. By the late 1950s they had developed a theology of mission that moved away from planting Disciples churches internationally, instead partnering with other Christian bodies already present to support God's mission in various countries. Thus today the mission of Global Ministries of the Christian Church (Disciples of Christ) is to receive and share the Good News of Jesus Christ by joining with global and local partners to work for justice, reconciliation and peace. This ecumenical way of missions explains why later chapters of this book focus primarily on cooperative missions around the world—though not neglecting the nationally led Disciples churches that grew out of Disciples missions in the Congo, Puerto Rico, and other nations.

RACE AND GENDER

The separation of the races both before and after the Civil War led to the development of African American churches and institutions among the Disciples. As early as the 1970s black churches began to organize into statewide conventions. Eventually black Disciples developed two major organizations, one of which continues as a separate denomination. That church—today called the General Assembly of the Church of Christ, Disciples of Christ, International—grew out of African American Churches in North Carolina that organized into Assembly in 1886. As their current name implies, they have missions in Liberia, Togo, Panama, Guyana, and other countries.

Preston Taylor

The second black organization grew out of an early organization named the National Convention of the Churches of Christ (NCCC), begun by Preston Taylor (1849–1931) and H. Malcolm Ayers in 1873. In 1917, Taylor and others formed the successor to the NCCC, the National Christian Missionary Convention, to work with black churches and ministries. That convention merged with the Christian Church (Disciples of Christ) in 1969, but retained its unique mission as the National Convocation of the Christian Church (Disciples of Christ) whose mission is "to provide an instrumentality within the structure of the Christian Church (Disciples of Christ) as a forum for the discussion of pertinent issues related to black church life in the context of total church life; for fellowship, program promotion, leadership training and such other general purposes as shall support and strengthen the congregations involved in the total mission of the church."

Two other general ministries of the Disciples focus on ethnic groups: the Central Pastoral Office for Hispanic Ministries and the North American Pacific/Asian Disciples (NAPAD). Like all Christians, Disciples continue to struggle with how to be genuine followers of Jesus in a racist world. At the General Assembly in 2001, they made becoming a pro-reconciling/anti-racist church a priority. At the congregational, regional, and general levels of the church, the church has begun initiatives to further that goal.

Disciples are also committed to gender equality. Early ordained ministers included Clara Hale Babcock (1850–1924), Sadie McCoy Crank (1863–1948), Bertha Mason Fuller (1876–1959), and Sara Lue Bostick (1968–1948). Important twentieth century leaders include Anna Atwater (1859–1941), the first woman vice-president of the United Christian Missionary Society, and Jessie M. Trout

(1895–1990) the founder of the Christian Women's Fellowship. A major milestone was the 2005 choice of Sharon E. Watkins as the first woman to serve as General Minister and President of the Christian Church (Disciples of Christ) and of a major American church body.

NUMERICAL DECLINE, IDENTITY, AND VISION

Disciples had about 1.7 million adherents in over 7800 churches in 1948. Between 1967 and 1972 about 750,000 adherents and 3500 congregations formally withdrew from the Disciples and formed the Christian Churches / Churches of Christ (see the next chapter). The Disciples Year Book reported 1,317, 044 members in 1975. The *2013 Yearbook and Directory of the Christian Church (Disciples of Christ)* reports a total membership of 600,330 with an average worship attendance of 184,491. This means there has been a significant decline in the number of Disciples in the last 40 years, with an average annual loss of over 18,000 members.

These numerical losses have caused the Disciples to make tough choices regarding their general ministries and have led to many discussions regarding the identity of the Christian Church (Disciples of Christ). In 2001 General Minister and President Richard L. Hamm (b. 1947) with input from many others, formulated the 2020 Vision of the Christian Church (Disciples of Christ). The 2001 General Assembly adopted the 2020 Vision, which contained four priorities to guide Disciples through the first two decades of the 21st century:

Sharon Watkins

- Becoming a Pro-reconciling /Anti-racist church
- Formation of 1,000 new congregations by 2020
- Transformation of 1,000 current congregations by 2020

77

- Leadership development necessary to realize these new and renewed congregations

In 2012 Disciples were already well over halfway toward the goal of planting 1000 new congregations.

QUESTIONS FOR DISCUSSION

1. What motivated Disciples to develop structures for ministry and mission? How have those structures furthered the mission of the church?

2. What is the significance of the name Christian Church (Disciples of Christ)? Why is it singular? What is the significance of the parenthesis?

3. How have Disciples been at the forefront of the ecumenical movement? How does this commitment to unity relate to both the past and the future of Disciples?

4. How did concept of mission change among Disciples in the twentieth century? What factors caused this change?

5. What is the greatest challenge facing Disciples in the last forty years?

6. What more can Disciples do to become a Pro-reconciling/ Anti-racist church?

FOR FURTHER READING

Foster, Douglas A., Newell Williams, Paul M. Blowers, and Anthony L. Dunnavant, eds. *The Encyclopedia of the Stone-Campbell Movement*. Grand Rapids, Michigan: Eerdmans, 2004. See article on Christian Church (Disciples of Christ).

Williams, Newell, Douglas Foster, and Paul Blowers. *The Stone-Campbell Movement: A Global History* St. Louis, Missouri: Chalice 2013. See pages 168–191.

Cummins, C. Duane. *The Disciples: A Struggle for Reformation.* St. Louis: Chalice Press, 2009.

Hamm, Richard L. *2020 Vision for the Christian Church (Disciples of Christ).* St. Louis: Chalice Press, 2001.

Kinnamon, Michael and Linn, Jan G. *Disciples: Reclaiming Our Identity, Reforming Our Practice.* St. Louis: Chalice Press, 2009.

Toulouse, Mark G. *Joined in Discipleship: The Shaping of Contemporary Disciples Identity.* St. Louis: Chalice Press, 1997.

Toulouse, Mark G., Gary Holloway, and Douglas A. Foster, *Renewing Christian Unity: A Concise History of the Christian Church (Disciples of Christ).* Abilene: Abilene Christian University Press, 2011.

Williams, D. Newell, ed. *A Case Study of Mainstream Protestantism: The Disciples' Relation to American Culture, 1880-1989.* Grand Rapids; Eerdmans, 1991.

Website

Christian Church (Disciples of Christ). http://www.disciples.org/.

Christian Churches and Churches of Christ

B etween 1967 and 1972 about 750,000 adherents and 3500 congregations formally withdrew from the Disciples and formed the Christian Churches and Churches of Christ. Some congregations use Christian Church in their name, others Church of Christ (not to be confused with the churches discussed in the next chapter). The plural "Churches" is significant since this group is organized congregationally with no official structure beyond the congregation.

AN EMERGING IDENTITY

The roots of this separation go back earlier to concerns that surfaced in the 1920s in the United States. To some extent, the division between Disciples and Christian Churches/Churches of Christ reflected the liberal-fundamentalist splits that occurred in several denominations in this era, with its focus on higher criticism of the Bible. Concern over "liberal" professors in some Disciples colleges led more conservative Disciples to form their own Bible colleges, like Cincinnati Bible Seminary in 1924.

However, among Disciples those concerns were mixed with differences over ecumenism, church organization, and mission work. While all Disciples supported the movement's emphasis on Christian unity, some felt that participation in church federations meant accepting the legitimacy of denominations that did not practice immersion, at least implying they must accept unimmersed

Christians as members of their local congregation. Others opposed this practice, known as "open membership."

This question was particularly relevant in international missions. Some American missionaries in China and the Philippines who were supported by the United Christian Missionary Society were accused of practicing open membership. The International Convention of the Disciples in 1920, 1922, and 1925 passed resolutions against open membership. However, the controversy continued and reflected a growing lack of confidence in the United Christian Missionary Society among many. Two camps formed among the Disciples, Cooperatives who supported the UCMS and Independents who supported missions independent of the UCMS.

DEVELOPING STRUCTURES

That mission support was largely through individual and direct congregational funding, but the independents soon developed other structures for promoting missions and for connecting churches. The Christian Restoration Association, founded in 1925, coordinated many mission efforts. The *Christian Standard* (published since 1866 and associated with the Christian Churches/Churches of Christ) reported widely on independent missions.

But it was the founding of the North American Christian

Convention (NACC) in 1927 that provided a structure and a rallying point for independents. From the beginning the NACC has been open to all with no official delegates, and makes no votes or resolutions. However, this annual event draws thousands for preaching, worship, and fellowship, providing a place where individuals and congregations can connect to dozens of parachurch mission and relief agencies (such as the Christian Missionary

Leonard Wymore

Fellowship). From 1961 to 1986,

Leonard Wymore (b. 1921) was Executive Director of the Convention. Another large gathering sponsored by members of Christian Churches/Churches of Christ is the National Missionary Convention founded in 1948 (now the International Conference on Missions).

As mentioned above, Christian Churches/Churches of Christ since the 1920s have also founded many Bible colleges many of which have grown into universities. These include: Alberta Bible College, Boise Bible College, Central Christian College of the Bible, Christian Kingdom College, Cincinnati Christian University, Dallas Christian College, Emmanuel Christian Seminary, Florida Christian College, Great Lakes Christian College, Hope International University, Colegio Biblico, Lincoln Christian University, Louisville Bible College, Manhattan Christian College, Maritime Christian College, TCM International Institute, Point University, Mid-Atlantic Christian University, Mid-South Christian College, Nebraska Christian College, Ozark Christian College, Saint Louis Christian College, Summit Christian College, and William Jessup University. These joined older Disciple institutions that came to identify with the Christian Churches/Churches of Christ: Milligan College (1880), Johnson University (1893), Northwest Christian University (1895), Crossroads College (1913), and Kentucky Christian University (1919).

DIVERSITY

The tensions between cooperatives and independents among Disciples intensified between the 1930s and 1960s, the period of restudy and restructure of the Disciples. As mentioned above, after 1972 the Christian Churches/Churches of Christ became a separate group from the Christian Church (Disciples of Christ). Still, several entities maintain ties between the two groups including the Pension Fund of the Christian Church, the Disciples of Christ Historical Society, the Stone-Campbell Dialogue, and the World Convention.

As is true in the other North American streams of the Stone-Campbell Movement, the views of members of the Christian Churches/Churches of Christ are not uniform. Some have

Dean Walker   James DeForest Murch

recognized three different mindsets in the group. One continues to emphasize the concept of restoration, connecting it with a conservative often inerrantist view of the Bible. R.C. Foster (1888–1970) of Cincinnati Bible Seminary is an early proponent of this view. Foster fought hard against biblical higher criticism, modern Bible translations, and church structure and bureaucracy.

A second approach, found among a majority of those in Christian Churches/Churches of Christ, finds common cause with American evangelicalism. One early leader with this view was James DeForest Murch (1892–1973). Murch promoted unity meetings among the cooperative and independent Disciples. He was an editor at the *Christian Standard* then became the editor of *United Evangelical Action,* the magazine of the National Association of Evangelicals. Beginning in the 1950s and 1960s, an increasing number of scholars in this group studied at Evangelical seminaries, some churches supported Billy Graham crusades, and eventually Evangelical speakers were on the program of the North American Christian Convention.

A third approach, still found today, was influenced by those like Dean E. Walker (1899–1988), Frederick D. Kershner (1875–1953), and Robert Fife (1918–2003) who sought to avoid division between cooperatives and independents. This group would emphasize restoration of the ideals of the New Testament as a matter of grace, the sacramental character of baptism and the Lord's Supper, and a Free Church polity open to unity with other Christians, all in the context of a believing but critical view of the Bible.

NUMERICAL GROWTH

From 1990 to 2010, Christian Churches and Churches of Christ were one of the fastest growing religious groups, gaining almost 20% in adherents. Possible reasons for that growth include aggressive evangelism, a conservative Bible-based message, and a generic name that appeals to those seeking a community church in a post-denominational era in the United States.

Part of that growth is tied to the rise of large congregations among the Christian Churches/Churches of Christ. In 2014 the *Christian Standard* reported 62 churches listed as megachurches (those with 2,000 or more in weekly attendance) and 62 listed as emerging megachurches (those with average attendance of 1,000 to 1,999). Three of those churches—Southeast Christian Church in Louisville, Kentucky, Central Christian Church in Henderson, Nevada, and Christ's Church of the Valley in Peoria, Arizona had over 20,000 in attendance and over 1000 baptized in a year.

As will be seen in later chapters, Christian Churches/Churches of Christ in the United States have been actively engaged in international mission work. As a result there are churches and ministries from this group in many countries throughout the world.

Questions for Discussion:

1. What do the terms "liberal" and "conservative" mean to you? Are these helpful descriptions? How do the terms "cooperatives" and "independents" play out in the division among the Disciples? Are these helpful terms?

2. Should congregations accept as members those who have not been immersed as believers? If not, does that mean we do not accept them as Christians?

3. What does "restoration movement" mean to you? Is this a helpful term?

4. Are those in Christian Churches/Churches of Christ Evangelicals? In what ways?

5. What contributions have the Christian Churches/Churches of Christ brought to the larger Stone-Campbell Movement?

6. Why do you think these churches are growing?

7. What are advantages of larger churches? Smaller churches?

For Further Reading

Foster, Douglas A., Newell Williams, Paul M. Blowers, and Anthony L. Dunnavant, eds. *The Encyclopedia of the Stone-Campbell Movement*. Grand Rapids, Michigan: Eerdmans, 2004. See article on Christian Churches/Churches of Christ.

Williams, Newell, Douglas Foster, and Paul Blowers. *The Stone-Campbell Movement: A Global* History. St. Louis, Missouri: Chalice 2013. See pages 84–89, 192–203.

Baker, William R., Editor. *Evangelicalism and the Stone-Campbell Movement. Vol. 1*. Downers Grove: InterVarsity Press, 2002.

Baker, William R., Editor. *Evangelicalism and the Stone-Campbell Movement. Vol. 2*. Abilene, Texas: Abilene Christian University Press, 2005.

Garrett, Leroy, *The Stone-Campbell Movement.* Joplin, MO: College Press, 1994.

Helsabeck, W. Dennis, Gary Holloway, Douglas A. Foster. *Renewal for Mission: A Concise History of the Christian Churches and Churches of Christ.* Abilene, Texas: Abilene Christian University Press, 2009.

North, James B. *Union in Truth: An Interpretive History of the Restoration Movement.* Cincinnati: Standard Publishing, 1994.

Webb, Henry E. *In Search of Christian Unity: A History of the Restoration Movement.* 2nd. Ed. Abilene, Texas: Abilene Christian University Press, 2003.

Website

Christian Church Today http://www.christianchurchtoday.com.

Christian Standard http://christianstandard.com/.

Churches of Christ

The 1906 Census of Religious Bodies recorded 159,658 members of Churches of Christ (by contrast, the Disciples of Christ had 982,701 members). The 1916 census reported 317,937 members, and the 1926 census 435,714 members in Churches of Christ. Even accounting for undercounts in the earlier censuses, the church more than doubled in a twenty-year period. This trend continued with estimates that the church grew to 600,000 by 1941.

Why such spectacular growth? Part of the reason is that the church was evangelistic. Not only traveling evangelists and local preachers but also ordinary church members felt the need to share their faith with others and plant new churches. Their message and methods also contributed to growth. The message was still the "simple gospel" made popular by Walter Scott. However, during this period Scott's five-finger gospel—faith, repentance, baptism, remission of sins, gift of the Holy Spirit, and eternal life—became a call to a five-step plan of salvation—hear, believe, repent, confess, and be baptized. The emphasis for many changed from responding to God's grace in order to receive God's promises to what humans must do to be saved. The method of having traveling evangelists speak in gospel meetings was also effective in a culture where there were few forms of popular entertainment to compete for attention.

COLLEGES

As with the Stone-Campbell colleges in the nineteenth century, colleges established by members of Churches of Christ also promoted and reflected the growth of the congregations. In 1891, James A. Harding (1848–1922) and David Lipscomb (1831–1917) started the Nashville Bible School (today known as Lipscomb University). Abilene Christian University (originally known as Childers Classical Institute) began in 1906 through the efforts of A.B. Barret (1879–1951), Jesse P. Sewell (1830–1924), and others. The school soon became a rallying point for churches in Texas, helping make the state a stronghold of Churches of Christ.

A. G. Freed (1863–1931) and N. B. Hardeman (1874–1965) founded what later became Freed-Hardeman University in 1908 (although the university traces its roots back to earlier colleges that date from 1869). Located in Henderson, Tennessee, the school soon became known for producing preachers in the mold of Hardeman. Harding College began in 1924 as a merger of two junior colleges, Arkansas Christian College and Harper College. In 1934, the school moved to its present location in Searcy, Arkansas. Businessman George Pepperdine (1886–1962) founded and endowed Pepperdine University in Los Angeles in 1937.

After World War II, the return of the veterans, the signing of the GI Bill giving them free education, and the growth of the postwar economy all created an increase in the number of Christian

Colleges and enrollment at those colleges. Members of Churches of Christ started several new schools during this era— Alabama Christian College (1942, renamed Faulkner University in 1985), Florida Christian College (1944, renamed Florida College in 1963), Oklahoma Christian College (1950), Columbia Christian College, Oregon (1956, reopened in 1994 as Cascade College under the control of Oklahoma Christian, then closed in 2009), York College,

N.B. Hardeman

Nebraska (1956), Lubbock Christian College, Texas (1957), Ohio Valley College, West Virginia (1958), Michigan Christian College (1959, renamed Rochester College in 1997), Northeastern Christian College, Pennsylvania (1959, merged with Ohio Valley College in 1993), and Crowley's Ridge College, Arkansas (1964).

BIBLE INTERPRETATION, ISSUES, AND DIVISIONS

By the 1880s, a new way of interpreting the Bible gained popularity, dominating Churches of Christ by the early twentieth century. Growing out of the controversies over instrumental music, the missionary society, Sunday Schools, and individual communion cups, this hermeneutic focused on what practices the Bible authorized.

Biblical authorization came through one of three ways: by direct command, apostolic example, and necessary inference. The biblical command to sing excluded instrumental music. An example in Acts authorized weekly communion. Multiple cups were allowed by a necessary inference from the command to commune (we are told to commune but not told how). Interestingly, those who opposed multiple cups or Sunday Schools used the same hermeneutic but disagreed on its application. Much of the theology of Churches of Christ was formed in controversy. Debating tended to push to extremes in doctrinal positions; one dared not admit that opponents were correct on any important point.

This narrow hermeneutic combined with a growing sectarianism led to several divisions in Churches of Christ in the twentieth century, primarily over whether the Bible authorizes practices like Sunday Schools, multiple cups in communion, premillennial teachings, and creating parachurch institutions like orphans homes, colleges, or nationwide media programs. One group of churches, insisting on a particularly aggressive form of evangelism and discipleship assumed a separate identity by the 1990s calling themselves the International Churches of Christ.

To a great extent, Churches of Christ were separatists for much of the twentieth century, remaining isolated from other professed followers of Christ, including others from the Stone-Campbell tradition. The story of one unity movement reflects this widespread

Batsell Barrett Baxter

attitude. In the 1930s, James DeForest Murch (1892–1973), a conservative member of the Disciples, and Claude Witty (1877–1952), a preacher for a Church of Christ in Detroit, led a series of unity discussions between leaders of the two groups. At the 1939 meeting in Indianapolis, H. Leo Boles (1874–1946), *Gospel Advocate* writer, told the Christian Churches that they were denominational, had left the faith, and would find the Churches of Christ where they had always been—based on the New Testament. His speech reflected the views of many in Churches of Christ and effectively put an end to the unity Movement.

As will be seen in the later chapters of this book, after the Second World War, Churches of Christ promoted international missions, growing from 46 missionaries sponsored by Churches of Christ in 1946 to 724 in 1967. In the same time period, two nationwide programs in the United States showed that Churches of Christ were becoming a force to reckon with in the larger culture. In 1952, the Highland Church of Christ in Abilene, Texas, took over the leadership of the "Herald of Truth" nationwide radio program, soon expanding it to include television. Highland was the program's sponsoring church with other congregations sending support (the same arrangement many churches had in missions). In 1959, Batsell Barrett Baxter (1916–1982) became the speaker on the television program, which made him for the next two decades the best-known member of Churches of Christ in the country.

The 1964–1965 New York World's Fair gave Churches of Christ another opportunity to make a nation-wide impression. The church's exhibit, housed in the Protestant Center, was in a central location and received much attention. Along with the exhibit, printed materials, a film presentation, and several evangelistic meetings introduced visitors to the church.

RACE

Race relations was one area where Churches of Christ failed to be counter-cultural. Like the society around them, the churches of this time were segregated. As a result, black Churches of Christ developed their own, in many ways separate, identity. Two great African-American church leaders emerged in this period. Marshall Keeble (1878–1968) was the great evangelist, baptizing more than 30,000 during his long ministry. G.P. Bowser (1874–1950) was an educator and editor, responsible for beginning several schools and a religious paper, the *Christian Echo,* to serve black Churches of Christ.

These two men had different approaches toward the white power structure of the church. Keeble in public claimed to see little racism among whites, always conducting himself the way that white culture expected—humbly and deferentially. As a result, he received praise from the church papers and financial support from prominent white church leaders. Bowser spoke out clearly against white racism and so worked almost exclusively with poor, black Christians. A turning point for Bowser came when he moved to Nashville in 1920 as principal of the Southern Practical Institute, a new school supported by Churches of Christ for African-American students. The white superintendent of the school, C.E.W. Dorris, insisted that the students enter the building by the back door, as the local culture dictated. Bowser called it racism and would have no part of it, leaving Nashville. The school closed in six weeks.

Sadly, all of the colleges established by members of Churches of Christ, except for Pepperdine, were racially segregated until the 1970s. As a result, members of Churches of Christ began two schools for African-American students. Nashville Christian Institute served black students at a secondary school level from 1940–1967. Southwestern Christian College, Terrell, Texas, began in 1950 and continues to serve students of all

Marshall Keeble

93

races today. Although he did not directly found either institution, both of these schools share the legacy of G.P. Bowser's efforts to educate black students among Churches of Christ.

While African-American evangelists like R.N. Hogan (1902–1997) boldly called the church to repentance and change concerning racism, there was an almost complete silence on the issue from the white leadership of the church. Even though black leaders in Churches of Christ, like Fred D. Gray (b. 1930) who served as lawyer for Rosa Parks and Martin Luther King, Jr. were influential in the Civil Rights Movement, when the church papers mentioned the Civil Rights movement, they generally condemned it as political, communist-inspired, or violent. Congregations split over how to care for orphans but were silent on racism. Why? Because we thought it absolutely necessary to be doctrinally correct on all the "issues" but otherwise followed the established culture. It was in this period that Churches of Christ became less of a movement— striving to restore the church—and became more of a settled church at ease in the Zion of America.

POLARIZATION—SECTARIAN AND NON-SECTARIAN

In 1966 and 1967, a new book and a new magazine signaled a change in Churches of Christ. The book was *Axe on the Root* by Ira Y. Rice, Jr. (1917–2001). In the combative style made popular earlier in this century, Rice attacked "liberalism" in Churches of Christ, particularly in educational institutions. In 1970, he began the monthly journal, *Contending for the Faith*, where he continued to name in bold print those he thought were leading the church away from its identity as the only Christians.

By contrast, in 1967 several leaders in Churches of Christ founded *Mission* magazine to be a voice of progressive thought. The magazine focused on searching for truth instead of assuming we had completely restored the New Testament church. *Mission* intentionally spoke to issues concerning the larger society—poverty, racism, and the Vietnam War—and called the church to rethink how we read the Bible and what we mean by restoration.

These publications reflected two radically different tendencies, a sectarian conservatism and a more open progressivism, a divide that would become more pronounced toward the end of the century. Through the 1960s and 1970s, the majority in Churches of Christ formed a large middle ground between the extremes, yet still tending toward the conservative end of the spectrum. Generally these churches continued the programs and perpetuated the attitudes of the post-war generation.

By the late 1960s, however, several scholars in Churches of Christ began to question whether the three-part hermeneutic (command, example, inference) could encompass all that was of relevance to Christians in Scripture. One of the most influential was Thomas H. Olbricht (1929–), a teacher at Abilene Christian University and Pepperdine University. Olbricht and others asked searching questions. Isn't it more biblical to emphasize the mighty acts of God in history? Should we not take the various types of literature in the Bible—poetry, law, prophecy, narrative, etc.—more seriously, using different interpretive approaches for each type?

The conservatives condemned this call for a more nuanced approach to understanding the Bible as a "New Hermeneutic." One important issue at stake in this discussion was the argument from silence. Biblical silence had been interpreted in various ways in our history. Thomas Campbell thought the silence of Scripture should not divide Christians. Later, the silence of the Bible on instrumental music and the missionary society was used to condemn those practices. In the noninstitutional controversy, the silence argument was used to condemn church support of colleges, orphans homes, and missionary-sponsoring congregations.

The broader approach to biblical interpretation treats silence neither as always prohibitive nor always permissive. Instead, the silence of Scripture concerning a specific practice calls for spiritual discernment. Does this practice reflect the nature of God? Is it in line with the biblical story of redemption? Does it build up the church? Does it promote or violate a clear principle of Scripture? This change makes it harder to identify the middle or even the extremes of Churches of Christ. The great uniformity among

Leroy Garrett

congregations in the 1940s and 1950s largely disappeared. Church papers, colleges, and well-known preachers have less of a unifying influence.

Many in Churches of Christ are less sectarian than fifty years ago. This is because of a broader biblical hermeneutic and a renewed appreciation for the heritage of unity in the Stone-Campbell Movement. Pioneers in moving Churches of Christ toward being nonsectarian were W. Carl Ketcherside (1908–1989) and Leroy Garrett (1918–) who moved in the late 1950s from a narrow sectarianism to work toward unity among all the streams of the Stone-Campbell Movement. In the 1980s, Rubel Shelly (1945–) who had been a leader among conservatives, came to embrace the movement's emphasis on unity, as shown in the title of his influential book, *I Just Want to Be a Christian.* Since then as a minister and educator, he has influenced many to practice nonsectarian Christianity.

In the last two decades, members of Churches of Christ have worked to unify the streams of the Stone-Campbell Movement through the Restoration Forums and the Stone-Campbell Dialogue, as well as engaging in a wider ecumenism through the World Convention, Christian Churches Together in the USA, the Faith and Order Commission, the National Council of Churches, the Global Christian Forum, and other ecumenical bodies.

A SPIRITUAL AWAKENING?

While there is concern about fragmentation among Churches of Christ, there are also encouraging signs of hope. One such sign is an increased emphasis on the work of the Holy Spirit. The charismatic revival of the 1970s had little direct effect on Churches of Christ, although a few congregations became charismatic and left the movement. It did force Churches of Christ to rethink their teaching on the Holy Spirit, a subject they had historically neglected. Some wanted to contain the Spirit completely in the Bible, but biblical study convinced most in the church that the Spirit lives in Christians and empowers them for service.

At the beginning of the new century, there were signs of a spiritual renewal. The younger generation especially showed more interest in and practice of the spiritual disciplines of prayer, study, and fasting. These younger Christians concern themselves more with Christian living and helping the poor than with the doctrinal disputes of a bygone era. In the words of a much earlier period, they wanted to "pray more and dispute less."

QUESTIONS FOR DISCUSSION

1. Why do you think Churches of Christ grew so much from 1906–1941?

2. How do Christian colleges promote cohesion among Churches of Christ? In what ways do they promote divisiveness?

3. What factors led many to believe that members of the Churches of Christ were the only Christians? Do many today still believe this?

4. What was the practice and attitude toward race relations in Churches of Christ until the late 1960s? Why was that the case? What can we learn from this part of our history?

5. Briefly describe what might be called the "conservatives" in Churches of Christ. What do they want Churches of Christ to be? How do they try to influence those in the church?

6. Briefly describe the "progressives" in Churches of Christ. What do they want Churches of Christ to be? How do they try to influence those in the church?

7. Why is there an increased awareness of and participation in the "spiritual disciplines" among members of Churches of Christ?

For Further Reading

Foster, Douglas A., Newell Williams, Paul M. Blowers, and Anthony L. Dunnavant, eds. *The Encyclopedia of the Stone-Campbell Movement*. Grand Rapids, Michigan: Eerdmans, 2004. See article on Churches of Christ.

Williams, Newell, Douglas Foster, and Paul Blowers. *The Stone-Campbell Movement: A Global* History. St. Louis, Missouri: Chalice 2013. See pages 76–84, 151–167.

Childers, Jeff W., Douglas A. Foster, and Jack R. Reese. *The Crux of the Matter: Crisis, Tradition, and the Future of Churches of Christ*. Abilene, Texas: Abilene Christian University Press, 2000.

Harrell, David Edwin, Jr. *The Churches of Christ in the 20th Century: Homer Hailey's Personal Journey of Faith*. Tuscaloosa: University of Alabama Press, 2000.

Hooper, Robert E. *A Distinct People: A History of Churches of Christ in the Twentieth Century*. West Monroe, Louisiana: Howard Press, 1993.

Hughes, Richard T. *Reviving the Ancient Faith: The Story of Churches of Christ in America*. Grand Rapids: Eerdmans, 1996.

Olbricht, Thomas H. *Hearing God's Voice: My Life with Scripture in Churches of Christ*. Abilene, Texas: Abilene Christian University Press, 1996.

Foster, Douglas A. *The Story of Churches of Christ*. Abilene, Texas: Abilene Christian University Press, 2013.

Website
Center for Restoration Studies, Abilene Christian University. http://wtda.alc.org/handle/123456789/30.

CHAPTER 9

Britain, the Commonwealth, and Europe

The Stone-Campbell Movement in Britain developed largely independently from the Movement in the United States, with little influence from Barton Stone but considerable influence from the writings of Alexander Campbell. The movement was never numerically large in Britain, but emigrants soon started churches in Canada, New Zealand and Australia. Missionaries from all of these countries planted churches throughout the world, particularly in Africa and Asia.

BRITAIN

Scotch Baptist minister William Jones in London, began to publish the *Millennial Harbinger and Church Advocate* in 1835, reprinting several articles from Alexander Campbell. James Wallis (1793–1867) of Nottingham was influenced by those writings and eventually led a group of Scotch Baptists to form the Church of Christ in Nottingham in 1836, the first Stone-Campbell church in Britain. Wallis became an early influential leader of the churches that numbered forty-three congregations and over 12,000 members by 1842 when the first Cooperation Meeting was held in Edinburgh. The churches continued to grow in spite of controversy over open membership and premillennialism.

David King (1819–1894) was the most significant second-generation leader in Britain, through his evangelistic work of planting churches in Manchester and Birmingham, through his journals, the *Bible Advocate*, then the *British Millennial Harbinger*, and through

David King

his voice in the Annual Meeting of the Cooperation. During King's time there was controversy over how close the British churches should be to the American movement, particularly with the Foreign Christian Missionary Society that was beginning to send evangelists to Britain. Many in Britain were troubled by what they saw as American practices like open communion, paid local pastors, colleges that trained preachers, and missionary societies.

As a result, in 1881 some more progressive churches formed the Christian Association that was closely connected with the American Foreign Christian Missionary Society. There were thus two groups of churches in Britain—the Association churches and the Cooperation churches—until they united in 1917.

The church faced several troublesome issues in the first half of the twentieth century. One was pacifism, the position of a majority of members during World War One, some of whom served prison time for their refusal to fight. Another involved education and higher criticism of the Bible. The churches had begun Overdale College in Birmingham in 1920 with William Robinson (1888–1963) as principal. Robinson was an influential theologian in the global Stone-Campbell Movement who defended higher criticism and worked ecumenically, attending the first Faith and Order Conference in Lausanne in 1927 and the first World Council of Churches meeting in Amsterdam in 1948. A third issue was that of having a local preacher or evangelist. The strong tradition in England was for mutual ministry that made many suspicious of evangelists coming from the United States with financial support.

These controversies led some British congregations to withdraw from the Annual Conference in 1924. Other congregations joined the dissenters through the years and they became known as the Old Paths churches. Later they became increasingly associated with Churches of Christ in the United States. Today they number about 70 churches with over 2300 members.

Those churches who were part of the Annual Conference continued to work together to promote unified fundraising and evangelistic work, appointing a General Secretary in 1948, and publishing an official magazine, the *Bible Advocate* and a hymnal. The Conference worked toward Christian union first with Baptists and later with Presbyterians and Congregationalists. In 1956 the Conference began to allow guest communion to the unimmersed and in 1972, guest (or ecumenical) membership. By 1978 the majority of the congregations supported union with the United Reformed Church. As a result, in 1980 the Annual Conference dissolved to allow each congregation to decide whether to join the United Reformed Church. Most did in 1981.

Great Britain

Those who did not join formed the Fellowship of Churches of Christ with their own conference structure. Springdale College in Birmingham, is associated with this group. There are 47 congregations with about 1200 adherents in the Fellowship.

CANADA

Churches that would become part of the Stone-Campbell Movement initially came to Canada through Scotch Baptists, Haldanes, and English Baptists who emigrated from Britain. John R. Stewart an immigrant from Scotland began the first church in Prince Edward Island in 1810 (a year before the Campbells began the Brush Run Church in the United States). These churches eventually developed their own identity as Churches of Christ or Disciples of Christ, organizing their first Cooperation Meeting in Norval, Ontario in 1843. Ontario was the numerical center of the movement and many from there planted churches in the Western Provinces during the last half of the nineteenth century. Perhaps the most influential leader in that century was David Oliphant, Jr. (1821–1885) who had studied under Alexander Campbell at Bethany and shaped the churches as an evangelist and an editor.

By the late 1880s there was a growing division in the Canadian churches similar to that in the United States. In 1901 there were 67 churches with 4711 members associated with the Disciples of Christ and 11 churches with 750 members associated with Churches of Christ. The Disciple churches organized the All-Canada Committee in 1922 to coordinate the work. In 1927 they formed the All-Canada College to train ministers; it later became a college without walls that provided funds for study at any university or seminary. When the Christian Church (Disciples of Christ) was formed in 1967, these churches became a regional expression of that church. They now number 22 churches and 1800 members.

Churches of Christ also spread into the Western Provinces in the 20th century. They founded Western Christian College in Saskatchewan in 1945, but after moving twice, the school closed in 2012. Great Lakes Christian College in Ontario is also associated with this group. The group includes 138 churches and over 7000 adherents. Christian Churches and Churches of Christ also have 62 churches with 9400 adherents in Canada. The influential Alberta Bible College, founded in 1932, is associated with them.

New Zealand

In 1844, Thomas Jackson from Scotland arrived in Nelson and established the first Church of Christ in New Zealand. In 1846, he and others formed a church in Auckland. From these beginnings other churches were planted, so that by the 1880s three district conferences were established that employed evangelists in their districts. By 1901 the first Dominion Conference met in Wellington. By 1905 there were 50 churches with 2400 members.

New Zealand churches began the College of the Bible at Glen Leith, Dunedin in 1927, with A.L. Haddon (1895–1961)

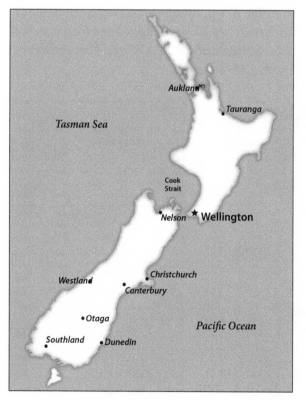

New Zealand

103

as its long-time principal. The school trained ministers and other workers until in closed in 1971. These churches always took the movement's emphases on evangelism and unity seriously, establishing missions around the world, particularly in Zimbabwe (see chapter 12).

But it was in the area of ecumenism that the New Zealand churches had influence beyond their numerical size. They were founding members of the National Council of Churches in New Zealand, had attendees at meetings of the World Council of Churches, and were members of the Joint Commission on Church Union that included Congregationalists, Methodists, Presbyterians, and Anglicans. Today eleven of their 33 congregations are part of union or cooperative parishes. These Associated churches (known today as Christian Churches NZ) have about 2000 members.

After World War II, missionaries from Churches of Christ in the United States came to New Zealand and formed new churches as well as the South Pacific Bible College. Those churches number about 25 with 1000 members.

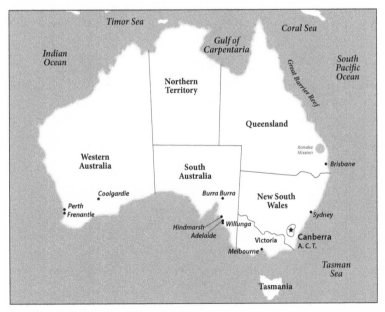

Australia

AUSTRALIA

In 1845 Thomas Magarey (1825–1902) and his family moved to Adelaide, South Australia from New Zealand. There they began the first Church of Christ in Australia in 1848. In New South Wales the church began in 1851 through the work of William Stinson and John Hodges, immigrants from England. In 1853, the first church in Victoria was begun around Melbourne. The Victorian churches grew and multiplied due to evangelism so that by

Alexander Russell Main

the mid-1860s there were twelve churches with a total of 230 members. At that time South Australia and New South Wales had three churches each.

As the congregations multiplied, cooperation meetings to promote evangelism were begun that grew into State Conferences in Victoria (1873), South Australia (1875), New South Wales (1885), Western Australia (1898), Tasmania (1894) and Queensland (1901). In 1906 the First Federal Conference was held.

In 1907, the Australian churches began the College of the Bible in Melbourne, relocated to the suburb of Glen Iris in 1910 when A.R. Main (1876–1945) became its principal. This school continues to train leaders for the churches. The campus was moved to Mulgrave (another Melbourne suburb) in 1989 and renamed the Church of Christ Theological College, being renamed again in 2011 as Stirling College after longtime principal Gordon Stirling (1914–2010).

From 1914 to 1941, A.R. Main also served as editor of the official paper of the Federal Conference, the *Australian Christian.*

The Australian churches began foreign missions in the 1880s, forming the General Foreign Missions Committee in 1891. Missionaries were sent to the New Hebrides (now Vanuatu), India, Japan, and Africa. The General Foreign Missions Committee eventually became the current Global Mission Partners who work with churches in Bangladesh, India, Indonesia, Papua New Guinea, South Sudan, Thailand, Vanuatu, Vietnam and Zimbabwe.

The Australian churches have also been influential in ecumenical work, first under the leadership of A.R. Main and then T.H. Scambler (1879–1944) who became principal of the school at Glen Iris in 1938. The Federal Conference in 1946 affiliated with the Australian Committee for the World Council of Churches.

Beginning in the 1940s there were tensions (but no overt divisions) among these Associated Churches on theological issues like critical views of Scripture and involvement in the ecumenical movement. This resulted in new schools in New South Wales, Western Australia, and Queensland. In 2002 the annual meetings of the Federal Conference ended, but a Federal Council of Churches of Christ in Australia meets biannually and appoints a Federal Coordinator. The Associated Churches of Christ today are organized by state and have 443 congregations with 36,500 adherents.

In the late 1940s missionaries from American Churches of Christ entered Australia and began planting churches, resulting today in 78 acapella churches with 1850 members.

EUROPE

The Foreign Christian Missionary Society sponsored three early missions to Europe. In 1876, A.O. Holck (1844–1907) moved from the United States to Copenhagen, planting a church in 1880. Jules and Annie DeLaunay came from the United States to France in 1877, settled in the Paris area, and evangelized until the mission was closed in 1886. Also in the 1880s, the Scottish Conference of the British Churches of Christ sent missionaries to Norway. Others worked in Norway, Denmark, and Sweden, supported by the Foreign Christian Missionary Society.

RUSSIA, UKRAINE, AND THE BALTICS

In Russia an indigenous movement known as the Gospel Christians arose in the 1870s led by Vasili Alexandrovich Pashkov (1830–1902). Around 1890, Ivan Stepanovich Prokhanov (1869–1935) assumed

Ivan Stepanovich Prokhanov and the Gospel Christians

leadership of the movement. In 1902 he visited the United States, came in contact with the Stone-Campbell Movement and began to align his churches with the movement. By 1926 the Gospel Christians claimed 600 missionaries and a membership of over 2 million. However, persecution under communism and isolation from the West during the Cold War reduced their numbers and their ties to the Stone-Campbell Christians. Today in western Russia, about 150 congregations with a total membership of around 3000 can be traced to them.

After the dissolution of the Soviet Union in 1991, many missionaries from Churches of Christ in America entered Russia and the Ukraine. Their work has resulted in one school for training Christian workers, the Christian Resource Center Russia in St. Petersburg, and in fifty-three churches in Russia and fifty in Ukraine.

Beginning in the 1990s, Churches of Christ planted churches in the Baltic States—Estonia, Latvia, and Lithuania—as well as in Belarus, Uzbekistan, and Kazakhstan.

Poland

In Poland another indigenous church movement developed led by Waclaw Zebrowski. In 1913, Disciples from the United States

107

visited him and his church in Warsaw, convinced many to be immersed, and formed a connection with the Stone-Campbell Movement. By 1930, those churches numbered 70 with a total of 6000 members.

In 1912 in Brooklyn, New York, Konstantin Jaroszewicz (1891–1984) was baptized. After attending Johnson Bible College in Knoxville, Tennessee, he returned to Poland in 1921 and began to plant churches, along with evangelists Jerzy Sacewitz (1903–1986) and Jan Bukowicz (1890–1950). These churches grew, survived the terrors of World War II and persecution under communism, and today number thirty-five churches with a total of 5000 members. In the 1950s they developed a working relationship with American Christian Churches /Churches of Christ through Polish Christian Ministries, founded by Paul and Adela Bajko. There are also three small acappella Churches of Christ in Poland.

GERMANY
Immediately after World War II, Otis Gatewood (1911–1999) and his family, with the support of several American Churches of Christ, entered Germany. From that time in 1947, over forty missionaries and thirty-eight German evangelists have planted churches in twenty-five cities with 4200 members, using radio and print to evangelize. These German churches have also sent workers to Poland, Ghana, Thailand, Pakistan, and India.

S. Scott Bartchy—Institute for the Study of Christian Origins

Earl Stuckenbruck (1916–2008) and family came to Tubingen, Germany in 1950, under the sponsorship of the European Evangelistic Society, associated with the Christian Churches/ Churches of Christ. They formed a church, published a paper, and in 1962 established the Institute for the Study of Christian Origins, which has served scholars from all expressions of the Stone-Campbell Movement. Twenty-two churches with 3200 members are a result of the work of the Stuckenbrucks and other evangelists.

AUSTRIA, SWITZERLAND, AND SOUTHEASTERN EUROPE

The work of Churches of Christ in Austria after World War II grew out of their Germany mission, when in 1956 the Bob Hare (1920–1995) family moved from Munich to Vienna. In 1958 Rudolph Rischer, a German converted by the Hares, began the church in Salzburg. By the 1970s there were six Churches of Christ in Austria. A similar story occurred in Switzerland where Heinrich Blum relocated from Germany in the early 1950s.

Christian Churches/Churches of Christ entered Austria through the mission of TCM, founded by Gene (1925–2007) and Lenora Dulin in Toronto, Canada. Their interaction with eastern European immigrants there moved them to relocate the mission to Vienna in 1971. After the fall of communism in Eastern Europe, TCM has focused more on training local ministers as TCM International Institute, currently with over 800 students. In 2010 TCMII merged with the European Evangelistic Association.

An indigenous "restoration movement" was formed under the leadership of Peter Poppoff in Bulgaria as early as 1909. In 1938, American Frank Vass (1880–1957) worked to plant churches in Romania, Czechoslovakia, Yugoslavia, and Hungary. By the time he returned to the United States in 1939, he had convinced eighty-five Baptist congregations to become part of the Stone-Campbell Movement.

After World War II American Churches of Christ sent Christian literature behind the Iron Curtain through the work of Eastern European Mission, founded by John Sudbury (1925–2010). In Croatia, Mladen Javanovic (1945–2013), a professor at the University of Zagreb, was baptized in 1971. Through his leadership, and the work of other evangelists, fourteen churches were planted and the Church of Christ in Croatia received official recognition from the government. He also was a founding leader of the Biblical Institute in Zagreb.

Europe

George Dumas from American Churches of Christ returned to his native Greece in 1960. Working with Antoni Roussos and others they planted churches in Greece and Rhodes. Albania, Bosnia, Hungary, Serbia, Slovakia, and Slovenia, all have at least one congregation of Churches of Christ.

ITALY

The Mediterranean Christian Mission from Christian Churches/ Churches of Christ sent Guy (1909–1984) and Thelma (1911–2008) Mayfield to Bari, Italy in 1947. In 1950 they relocated to Rome. Other missionaries joined them working in other areas in Italy resulting today in twenty congregations with 500 members.

Cline Paden (1919–2007) from American Churches of Christ came to Naples in 1949 and immediately faced strong opposition to his ministry from some Catholic groups. By 1960, thirty missionaries were working in Italian cities, establishing training schools in Florence and Milan, local lectureships, an orphanage, magazines, and radio work. Today there are 2000 members of these churches in sixty-four congregations.

THE NETHERLANDS, BELGIUM, AND FRANCE

While living in the United States in 1942, Jacob Vandervis was convinced to leave the Church of Jesus Christ of Latter Day Saints and to join the Churches of Christ. In 1946 he returned to his native Netherlands and planted churches, eventually joined by more than sixty missionaries in the last few decades of the century.

In Belgium, Samuel F. (1918–2009) and Maxine (1918–2012) Timmerman arrived from Churches of Christ in 1948. Soon other couples came and planted twenty churches in the French and Flemish areas.

In 1949, the Maurice Hall and Melvin Anderson families, also from United States Churches of Christ, moved to Paris. By 1960, twenty-one workers and families had joined them. In spite of the difficulty in establishing local French leadership, today there are nine churches with a total of 400 members in France.

SPAIN AND PORTUGAL

Churches of Christ in Spain owe their existence to an encounter between Juan Antonio Monroy (b. 1929) and those at the Church of Christ exhibit at the New York World's Fair in 1964. Monroy had already begun an evangelical reform movement in Spain. As a result of his contact in New York, he was asked by Churches of Christ to broadcast a version of the Herald of Truth radio program in Spain. Churches of Christ supported many Spanish evangelists so that today there are around 2500 members in thirty churches.

Churches of Christ initially came to Portugal through American missionaries in Brazil, Arlie and Alma Smith, who moved to Lisbon from Brazil in 1969. Dick and Sarah Robinson from Christian Churches/Churches of Christ arrived through the Portugal Christian Mission in 1982. In 1988, they were joined by Roberto and Delani Fife from Brazil. This mission continues to be supported by churches in the United States and Brazil.

FRATERNAL WORKERS

In addition to the countries above, Stone-Campbell churches are also found in Ireland, Iceland, Gibraltar, Luxembourg, Malta, and Moldova. From the stories above, it is clear that most Stone-Campbell missions in Europe began after World War II, when the continent was recovering from the war's devastation. Widows, orphans, and refugees particularly needed help. All the missions mentioned above offered compassionate assistance. Disciples of Christ worked through Church World Service and other agencies to send assistance. Because of their commitment to ecumenism, Disciples did not plant new churches in Europe but partnered with existing churches. One program that has born much fruit is that of sending "fraternal workers" from the United States to work with European churches to share resources and deepen understanding.

It is also clear from the stories above that Stone-Campbell churches are not numerous in Great Britain, Canada, New Zealand, Australia, and Europe. This may be because of secularization and low church attendance found in all Christian groups in those areas. What has characterized the churches in these places is a strong emphasis on education, with schools and colleges being formed in almost every country. Interestingly, some in these churches have been at the forefront of ecumenical efforts locally, nationally, and globally, while others continue to be quite narrow in their view of who is a Christian. However, the faithful service of missionaries and immigrants, not just from the United States but from Brazil, Africa, and other places, continues to bear fruit.

Questions for Discussion

1. Churches in Great Britain were influenced by the writings of Alexander Campbell but knew little of Barton Stone. From what you know of these two men, how has the Campbell (but not Stone) influence shaped British churches?

2. What is the importance of schools established in the countries in this chapter? What were the purposes of those schools?

3. What do you think about the indigenous movements in this chapter who were working and worshipping in ways similar to Stone-Campbell movement churches even before contact with those churches? What does that say about the Stone-Campbell approach to the church?

4. Why has it been so difficult to cultivate local leadership of churches in many parts of Europe?

5. What is the better approach to evangelism, to plant new Stone-Campbell churches or to work ecumenically with existing churches? Why?

For Further Reading

Foster, Douglas A., Newell Williams, Paul M. Blowers, and Anthony L. Dunnavant, eds. *The Encyclopedia of the Stone-Campbell Movement*. Grand Rapids, Michigan: Eerdmans, 2004. See articles on Australia, the Movement in; Europe, Missions in; Great Britain and Ireland, Churches of Christ in; New Zealand, the Movement in.

Newell Williams, Douglas Foster, and Paul Blowers. *The Stone-Campbell Movement: A Global History*. St. Louis, Missouri: Chalice 2013. See pages 94–114, 344–366.

Great Britain

Nisbet, Joe. *Historical Survey of Churches of Christ in the British Isles*. Aberdeen Scotland: 2000.

Thompson, David Michael. *Let Sects and Parties Fall: A Short History of the Association of Churches of Christ in Great Britain and Ireland*. Birmingham, England: Berean Press, 1980.

Watters, A.C. *History of British Churches of Christ*. Indianapolis: School of Religion, Butler University, 1948.

Website
Churches of Christ (Christian Worker) http://www.christian-worker.org.uk/.

Fellowship of Churches of Christ http://www.fellowshipcc.co.uk/.

CANADA
Muir, Shirley L. *Disciples in Canada 1867-1967*. Indianapolis, Indiana: World Outreach Education Dept., United Christian Missionary Society, 1966.

Website
Canadian Churches of Christ Historical Society. http://ccchs.ca/.

Christian Church (Disciples of Christ) in Canada http://www.canadadisciples.org/.

AUSTRALIA
Chapman, Graeme. *One Lord, One Faith, One Baptism: A History of the Churches of Christ in Australia*. 2nd edition. Melbourne: Vital Publications, 1989.

Roper, David. *Voices Crying in the Wilderness: a History of the Lord's Church with Special Emphasis on Australia*. Adelaide, Australia: Restoration Publications, 1979.

Website
Churches of Christ in Australia. http://cofcaustralia.org/.

Global Mission Partners. http://www.inpartnership.org.au/.

NEW ZEALAND
Christian Churches New Zealand http://www.ccnz.org/.

EUROPE

Ellis, Geoffrey H. and Wesley L. *The Other Revolution: Russian Evangelical Awakenings*. Abilene, Texas: Abilene Christian University Press, 1996.

Bajko, Paul. *A History of the Churches of Christ in Poland*. Bel Air, Maryland: Polish Christian Ministries, 2001.

Gatewood, Otis, *Preaching in the Footsteps of Hitler*. Nashville, Tennessee: Williams Printing, 1960.

Monroy, Juan Antonio, *Juan Antonio Monroy: An Autobiography*. Abilene, Texas: Abilene Christian University Press, 2011.

Website

Eastern European Missions. http://www.eem.org/.

Global Ministries, Christian Church (Disciples of Christ) http://globalministries.org/mee/partners/.

TCMI International Institute. http://www.tcmi.org/.

Asia and the Pacific Islands

S ome of the earliest international mission work done by churches in the United States, Great Britain, and Australia focused on Asia. Today Stone-Campbell Christians on the continent number at least one half million and perhaps more than two million in vibrant, growing churches.

INDIA AND PAKISTAN

In 1882 the Foreign Christian Missionary Society and the Christian Women's Board of Missions, both from American Disciples, sent eight missionaries to Bombay (Mumbai): Greene L. (1846–1906) and Emma (d. 1922) Wharton, Albert (1847–1922) and Mary Kelly Norton, Ada Boyd (d. 1915), Laura Kinsey (d. 1926), Mary Graybiel (1846–1935), and Mary Kingsbury (1857–1926). They soon moved the mission to Harda and were joined by other missionaries in the Disciples India Mission, establishing schools, clinics, publishing houses, and orphanages. By 1907 there were eleven new mission stations and fifty-nine additional missionaries. Through the India Christian Missionary Society they developed Indian evangelists like Hira Lal (1875–1955) and his wife Sunarin Bai (d. 1952) in

Hira Lal and Sunarin Bai

117

Mungeli. This began a process of indigenization of the Indian mission, shown by the founding of the India Disciples Church Council in 1915.

In 1905 Australian Churches of Christ established a mission in Baramati with the Henry Strutton family. Earlier, Australian Mary Thompson served with the Harda mission. Joined by fifteen missionaries and twenty-six Indian evangelists in the 1920s, they formed the Conference of Churches of Christ in West India in 1927. For the next sixty years Edna Vawser (1902–1994) and Hazel Skyce were leaders of the Conference. Today that work is still assisted by Global Mission Partners of the Australian Churches of Christ. In 1925 the Australian Churches of Christ opened the Dhond mission station that included a hospital led by Dr. G.H. Oldfield.

The Foreign Missionary Committee of British Churches of Christ supported the mission of Paul Singh in Daltonganj beginning in 1909. G.P. Pittman soon joined the mission, supported by

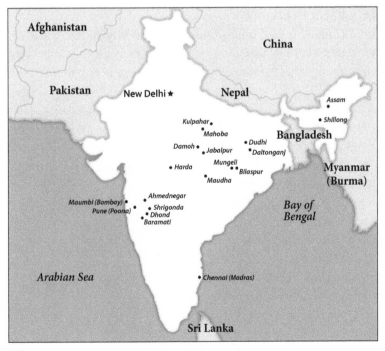

India

Australian churches. Two other mission stations were soon opened through the work of indigenous evangelists.

Indigenization continued to grow throughout the 1920s with Indian leaders like Alfred Aleppa (d. 1947) in Damoh, Harrison Singh (trained at Hiram College in the United States) at Barela and later others like Luther Shuh, Samuel Massih, and Peter Solomon. By the mid 1960s the United Christian Missionary Society missions were almost completely governed and supported by Indians.

The process of ecumenical union also grew from the 1920s to the 1960s. Encouraged by the United Christian Missionary Society (UCMS) and by most British and Australian Churches of Christ, the majority of Indian Churches of Christ supported ecumenical cooperation and eventually joined in the formation of the United Church of North India in 1970.

UCMS missionaries Sterling (1886–1928) and Dr. Zoena (1882–1979) Rothermel came to oppose some policies of the Society as discussed in chapter seven. They continued their work in India, but as direct support missionaries, later associated with Christian Churches/Churches of Christ. Some other missionaries followed the Rothermels into direct support missions. Vijai (1933–1993) and Pushpa Lall had served in a UCMS mission but became direct support missionaries. Their son Ajai and his wife Indu started the Central India Christian Mission in 1982 that today serves thousands yearly in evangelistic and compassion ministries. Other new efforts arose like the Benevolent Social Services of India begun in 1970 by Canadians David (1910–1976) and Lois (1916–2006) Rees, who had served in India since 1953. Missionaries from India and from the United States have planted churches in Nepal, Bhutan, Sri Lanka, and Bangladesh.

American Churches of Christ sent the Edward S. Jelley (1878–1962) family to Bombay in 1911. Three other couples soon joined them; however, the unity of this mission was broken by controversy over premillennialism. In 1925 the George Desha family moved to Bombay to continue the mission but soon moved to Darjeeling. They returned to the United States in 1927. Churches of Christ did not return to India until 1963 through the work of Canadians John

119

Carlos (1903–2001) and Myrtle Bailey, first at Shillong, then at Madras. By 1972, with the help of Indian evangelists like the brothers Nehemiah and Joshua Gootnam, over 700 churches had been planted in the area. Indian Churches of Christ established the Madras School of Preaching (now the National Bible College) in 1969. Many short-term workers from the United States came to assist Indian evangelists. Ron and Karen Clayton, missionaries in India for over 30 years, have kept detailed records of congregations and baptisms and list 48,880 Churches of Christ in India with a combined membership of 1,139,562 today.

American Church of Christ missionaries Gordon and Jane Hogan came to Lahore, Pakistan in 1961. Other missionaries followed but most left the country by the late 1960s. Pakistani evangelists like Anwar Masih, Hadayat H. Din, and Asgar Ali carried on the mission, resulting in twenty-five churches with 750 adherents today.

The Lee Turner family from Christian Churches/Churches of Christ was in Lahore in the early 1960s. Pakistani Saleem Massey graduated from Cincinnati Bible Seminary and returned to his country in 1989 and started Pakistan Christian Evangelical Services. With support from churches in the United States, Scotland, and Australia, he and others have planted eight churches with more than 3,000 members.

CHINA, TAIWAN, AND TIBET
Along with India, China was another early mission of the Foreign Christian Missionary Society. In 1886 it sponsored Canadian Dr. William Macklin (1860–1947) as a missionary to Nanking. Edwin P. Hearnden (d. 1896) and Albert F. H. Saw (1865–1898) from Britain soon joined the mission along with two couples from the United States. They began medical work, schools, and other mission stations assisted by converts like Shi Kwei-biao (d.1925) and additional missionaries including Rosa Tonkin from Australian Churches of Christ. These missions persevered under Chinese opposition to "foreign" influences, through the Boxer Uprising of 1898–1901, and during Sun Yat-sen's republican revolution of 1911–1912. By the 1920s the missionaries began to relinquish con-

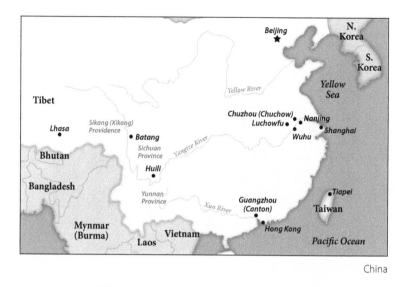

China

trol to Chinese Christian leaders like Li Hou-fu (d.1939) the co-secretary of the mission.

Chinese leadership was essential in preserving the churches through the trying political situation of the next few decades. Japanese occupation of China began in 1937 with the brutal "rape of Nanking" where missionaries Miner Searle Bates (1897–1978) and Minnie Vautrin (1886–1941) protected thousands of innocent lives. During the occupation, Shao Ching-San (d. 1958), known as Luther Shao, who completed a Ph.D. at Yale in 1934, returned to China and became secretary of the mission. Due to Communist rule beginning in 1949 the last of the United Christian Missionary Society workers left in 1951.

American Churches of Christ entered China through the work of George (1898–1991) and Sallie (1896–1981) Benson in Hong Kong beginning in 1925. By 1930 they had established a mission in Canton on the Chinese mainland with schools and religious papers. Lowell (1910–2007) and Odessa (1911–2010) Davis and others joined them, but were forced to return to Hong Kong during the Japanese occupation. They briefly returned to Canton in 1947–1949, but left again during the communist takeover. In 1949, Elizabeth Bernard and others from American Churches of Christ

121

Albert Shelton (1920)

revived the Hong Kong mission, establishing churches and preaching schools, so that today there are around 400 members. In 1959, Roy Mullinax, and Enoch B. and Jeanine Thweatt moved to Taipei. Several missionaries have since served in Taiwan, planting nine congregations.

Global Ministries of the Christian Church (Disciples of Christ) has worked ecumenically in China particularly in education of church leaders and in economic development in rural communities.

In Tibet, Dr. Susie Rijnhart (1868–1908) from Canada began work in 1894. In 1906 the United Christian Missionary Society began support of Dr. Albert Shelton (1875–1922) and others in Batang. The mission expanded to Chamdo and included a school, hospital, and orphanage. The death of Shelton at the hand of robbers in 1922 caused an outpouring of financial support for the mission resulting in seven additional missionaries arriving by 1923. However, by 1935, the United Christian Missionary Society had decided to close the mission. Even before that, the controversy over open membership had caused missionaries J. Russell (1898–1991) and Gertrude (1896–1977) Morse to resign from the UCMS mission and seek direct support. By World War II they and others had established thirty churches with a total of 6000 members. Other direct support missionaries came in the late 1930s to revive the mission in Batang, including its medical, agricultural, and orphanage programs. However, the Chinese communist annexation of Tibet begun in 1950 forced the missionaries to flee to other Asian countries.

JAPAN

In 1883, the Foreign Christian Missionary Society sent George T. (1843–1920) and Josephine (1950–1995) Smith and Charles E. (1853–1898) and Laura Garst (1861–1925) to Japan where they settled eventually in Akita. By 1889 they had formed a church, and were joined by six other missionaries. Relocating the mission to Tokyo in 1890, by 1899 they had twelve mission stations, ten local evangelists, a school, and churches with 611 members. By 1909 twenty-four more missionaries had arrived. In 1903 Drake Bible College was founded that later merged with other schools to form Tokyo Union Theological Seminary. However, the Great Depression caused the withdrawal of all but two missionary couples and the reduction to four stations in Akita, Tokyo, Fukushima, and Osaka. In 1940, under pressure from the Japanese government,

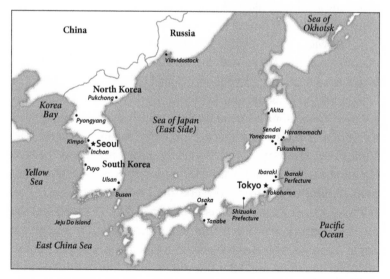

Japan and Korea

123

Yunosuke Hiratsuka

most of those churches joined with thirty-four Protestant denominations to form the United Church of Christ in Japan (Kyodan). Today the Christian Church (Disciples of Christ) partners with the Kyodan in evangelism, education, and social services.

What eventually became the direct support Yotsuya mission began in Tokyo in 1892 with missionary W.K Asbill, assisted by Kakujiro Ishikawa, Lucia Scott, Carme Hostetter, and Alice Miller. Later leaders William D. (1864–1936) and Emily (1873–1953) Cunningham expanded the mission. Most of the churches from this mission did not join the United Church of Christ in Japan (Kyodan). During World War II all the missionaries were evacuated. After the war, many missionaries arrived from Christian Churches/Churches of Christ to reestablish the mission, opening Tokyo Bible Seminary in 1948. In the 1950s the mission took steps to transfer leadership to Japanese Christians. Today there are over sixty churches with 9600 members that have a heritage in this mission.

John Moody McCaleb (1861–1953) from American Churches of Christ came to Tokyo with the Azbill mission in 1892, but soon began work separately. Eventually joined by missionaries from the United States, Canada, and Australia, by 1920 this mission consisted of twenty-one house churches in the Tokyo area, along with schools and religious papers. One early Japanese leader was Yunosuke Hiratsuka (1873–1953) who preached at the Kamitonizaka Church of Christ for over forty years. In the 1920s, Sarah Andrews (1892–1961), and the brothers Herman J. Fox (1896–1960) and Harry Robert Fox, Sr. (1896–1974) joined the mission. During World War II all the missionaries left except for Sarah Andrews who was too sick to travel and lived under house arrest for the duration. After the war, at least fifteen missionaries from Churches of Christ returned, evangelizing through gospel meetings, radio, and print, so that by 1951 there were more than twenty-four churches, as well as homes to assist orphans, the blind, and the elderly. In 1948 the churches began a school system that grew into Ibaraki Christian University. Today there are 60 churches and 1000 members of these Churches of Christ.

KOREA

The Stone-Campbell Movement entered Korea through the Yotsuya Japan mission when William Cunningham sent Lee Wan Kyun there in 1924, and Lee In Pom in 1933. By 1940, they and others had planted twelve churches with 5000 members. In 1936 John (1905–1987) and Wahneta (1901–2002) Chase, who had been missionaries to Japan, founded the Korean Christian Mission. By 1940 that mission had six churches led by Koreans. During World War II the Japanese government (which controlled Korea) tried to force Shinto worship on Korean Christians, and also prohibited Koreans from receiving financial support from foreigners. The Chase family left during the war but returned with John J. Hill (1913–2009) and other missionaries in 1946 to rebuild churches and begin Korean Christian Bible Seminary. These churches survived during the Korean War (1950–1953) so that in 1953 the Korean Christian Mission had 51 churches and 1905 members.

From the 1960s on there was a movement toward autonomy for the Korean churches. Eventually Korean leaders formed the Conference of Christian Churches and Churches of Christ. One influential leader was Chae Yoon Kwon who, after study at San Jose Bible College and Lincoln Seminary, returned to Korea to plant churches, begin a publishing house, establish a children's home, and with others found Korea Christian Seminary (later Seoul Christian University). Over 271 churches are in this Conference.

Dong Suk Kee (1881–1971), who studied at Cincinnati Bible College but became associated with American Churches of Christ, entered Korea in 1930. By 1940 he and others had begun seven churches in what later became North Korea. Kang Myung Suck also

Dong Suk Kee

affiliated with Churches of Christ while a student in the United States and returned to Korea in 1936 to start churches in Ulsan, Seoul, and Inchon. All of these churches faced the difficulties of Japanese occupation, World War II, and the Korean War. By the 1960s seven missionaries had arrived from American Churches of Christ, had founded Korean Christian University, and planted churches throughout Korea. Eventually leadership of the churches passed completely to Koreans. Today those churches number 104 with 5000 members.

The Christian Church (Disciples of Christ) works in Korea through several ecumenical partners. Korean Disciples like Guenhee Yu, have provided leadership for the North American Pacific/Asian Disciples, a general ministry of the Christian Church that serves those Disciples in the United States and in other countries.

In keeping with the Stone-Campbell heritage, prayer, evangelism, and unity are priorities of the Korean churches. One practice common to most Christians in Korea is gathering daily for morning prayer. South Korean churches have sent missionaries to North Korea, Russia, China, and parts of Asia, Latin America, and Africa. The instrumental and non-instrumental congregations increasingly cooperate in efforts such as education and translation and publishing Stone-Campbell materials for use in the churches.

PHILIPPINES
The Foreign Christian Missionary Society sent Herman Williams (1872–1958) and W.H. (1872–1948) and Elinor (1876–1947) Manna to Manila in 1901. They soon relocated to Laong, were joined by other missionaries, and by 1913 had begun several mission stations, hospitals, and a college. By 1922 there were twenty-five missionaries and 9,289 members of the churches. The Great Depression, however, caused the withdrawal of all but two

missionaries by 1932. Japan invaded in 1941 and by 1943 had forced many churches into the union church—the Evangelical Church of the Philippines. After World War II other missionaries came from the United Christian Missionary Society to assist and rebuild. In 1948, the churches joined the United Church of Christ in the Philippines, with one of their own, Enrique Sobrepena, elected as its founding bishop.

In 1926, missionaries Leslie and Carrie Wolfe returned to the Philippines. They had broken with the Foreign Christian Missionary Society over comity agreements and charges of open membership, choosing to be funded by direct support coordinated by the Christian Restoration Association. They soon organized most of the churches in the Manila area into the Christian Convention. Under Filipino leaders including Ligoria Carmona, H. M. Mayor, and Faustino Peneyra, over ninety churches had been established by 1950. In more recent decades, those churches have seen phenomenal growth with Diego Romulo as leader, now with over 1200 churches and 200,000 adherents. Other missionaries from the Christian Churches/Churches of Christ have worked in the Philippines, planting churches and founding schools and seminaries.

H. G. and Marie Cassell from American Churches of Christ reached the Philippines in 1928, after George Benson made a brief evangelistic visit there from his work in China. By the 1950s, over a dozen missionaries were in the country, beginning fourteen schools, like Philippine Bible College in 1948, for training local ministers. Today churches from those missions, now under local leadership, number 700 with 40,000 members.

BURMA, THAILAND, AND SOUTHEAST ASIA

1892 marked the beginning of the Burma mission of the British Foreign Missionary Committee, when Robert (1864–1933) and Agnes (d. 1894) Halliday and A. E. Hudson landed at Ye. The work was difficult with the first convert made in 1895. By 1905 other missionaries had arrived, working particularly in education, but by 1910 the work had been suspended.

Enrique Sobrepena

The Hallidays joined the work of the Foreign Missionary Committee in Nakhon Pathom, Siam (now Thailand). That mission began in 1903 with Percy (1879–1957) and Mary Clark, soon assisted by Thai evangelists like Chun Kwang and Ki Hong. They not only planted churches in various languages—Thai, Chinese, and Mon—but also began education and medical work. During the Japanese invasion in World War II, the Clarks were interred in POW camps. In 1951 the British Churches of Christ transferred the mission to the Disciples United Christian Missionary Society. At one time missionaries from the United States, Great Britain, and China worked with local Thai evangelists. In 1962 the mission transferred all property to the indigenous Church of Christ in Thailand, although Disciples like Victor and Marian McAnallen and Allan and Joan Eubank among others continue to serve as fraternal workers in Thailand.

Christian Churches/Churches of Christ missionaries C. W. and Lois Callaway came to Thailand from work in China in 1949. The work in Thailand was given a boost when Eugene and Robert Morse relocated the North Burma Christian mission to Northern Thailand in 1973. Also Russell LaVerne Morse began Asia Christian Services with radio, literature, and medical aid. Twenty churches with 2600 members are today associated with Christian Churches/ Churches of Christ. Missionaries from American Churches of

128

Christ Parker and Donna Henderson began work in Bangkok in 1958. In 1971, Chai and Sue Voraritskul became influential leaders among the churches that now number 100 with 2000 members. Churches of Christ also began evangelism in Singapore when Ira Y. Rice, Jr. arrived in 1955. The churches there began Four Seas College, led for years by dean Tan Keng Koon (1924–1979), training evangelists who planted churches in Singapore, Malaysia, and Indonesia. In the 1960s Churches of Christ initiated Operation Saigon with Maurice and Marie Hall arriving in 1964, followed soon by thirteen other missionaries. Eventually seventeen churches were planted, but by 1975 all the American workers had been evacuated due to war. Churches of Christ also did limited work in Laos and Cambodia beginning in the 1990s.

Vanuatu, Papua New Guinea, and the Pacific Islands

Willie Tabimancon, while a worker in Australia, was converted by John Thompson. Returning to his home on Pentecost Island in the New Hebrides (now Vanuatu) in 1901, he began to evangelize, so that when Thompson came for a mission visit in 1903 he found over fifty people ready for baptism. One of those converts, Peter Pentecost, began to preach on Aoba Island, forming a church in 1903. On Maewa Island, there were as many as 2000 members of the churches by 1900. Australian Churches of Christ sent several missionaries to the islands to assist local teachers like Abel Barni. In the 1940s they sent medical workers like Mary Clipston and Violet Wakely, and also founded schools and Bible colleges. By 1980, the churches and institutions were led by local leaders under the organizational name of the Vanuatu Conference of Churches of Christ. Today they number over ninety-two churches with over 8000 members, making Vanuatu the country with the highest percentage of Stone-Campbell Christians per capita. They have sponsored missions to Papua New Guinea, the Solomon Islands, New Caledonia, and Fiji.

In 1958 the Overseas Mission Board of the Australia Churches of Christ sent Frank Beale and Harold Finger to Papua New Guinea. By the 1960s the board sponsored more than twenty missionaries in six villages, working in evangelism, education, and medical services. In the 1970s the board began to transfer leadership to local leaders who eventually formed the Melanesian Evangelical Churches of Christ, today with 112 congregations and 6000 members. American Churches of Christ came to Papua New Guinea in the 1970s through the work of Joe and Rosabelle Cannon and others, resulting in a hundred churches with 5000 members today. In 1977, Al Hamilton of Christian Churches/Churches of Christ began Pioneer Bible Translators that has sent more than seventy-five missionary-translators to Papua New Guinea.

American Churches of Christ also have churches in Fiji, Guam, French Polynesia, Tonga, American Samoa, Micronesia, Tuvalu, Kiribati, the Marshall Islands, and Northern Mariana. Robert and Mary Martin have worked in many of these countries.

THE MIDDLE EAST
The first mission of the American Christian Missionary Society in Jerusalem from 1850 left no church. In 1960, Ralph Henley and Ernest Stewart from American Churches of Christ began work with both Jews and Palestinians in Jerusalem. One of their converts was Joe Shulam, who leads a Messianic synagogue in Jerusalem today. Several American and Palestinian workers began churches in Ramallah, Nazareth, and Eliaboun.

Churches of Christ have also done evangelistic work in Jordan, Egypt, Lebanon, Kuwait, Turkey, Afghanistan, Iraq, Bahrain, Saudi Arabia, the United Arab Emirates, and Cyprus. In most of those countries there are small house churches, primarily of American members of the military.

While Stone-Campbell Movement churches are few and small in the Middle East, the number and size of those churches in Asia is growing significantly. Even so, Christians of any kind are a small percentage of the population in most Asian countries. Because of their minority status many Christians, including those in the Stone-Campbell Movement, face discrimination and even violent persecution for their faith. That minority status has led many to embrace other Christians and work for Christian unity. It also has produced thoughtful and gracious encounters with Hindus, Muslims, Buddhists, and followers of other non-Christian religions.

QUESTIONS FOR DISCUSSION

1. What countries sent missionaries to India? To China? To Papua New Guinea? What does this tell us about the mission impulse in the Stone-Campbell Movement?

2. Stone-Campbell Churches joined union churches in many of these Asian countries. Was it easier to have church unions in Asia than it has been in the United States? Why or why not?

3. What challenges and hardships have missionaries and local church workers faced in some of these countries? How did they react to those difficulties?

4. Besides planting churches, what other types of work were done by missionaries and local workers in this chapter? How did that work further evangelism?

5. What did you find most surprising or significant in this chapter?

FOR FURTHER READING

Foster, Douglas A., Newell Williams, Paul M. Blowers, and Anthony L. Dunnavant, eds. *The Encyclopedia of the Stone-Campbell Movement*. Grand Rapids, Michigan: Eerdmans, 2004. See articles Asia, Missions in; Korea, the Movement in.

Williams, Newell, Douglas Foster, and Paul Blowers. *The Stone-Campbell Movement: A Global History* St. Louis, Missouri: Chalice 2013. See pages 118–133, 254–284.

MISSIONS

Bowes, Keith. *Partners: One Hundred Years of Mission Overseas by Churches of Christ in Australia, 1891–1991*. North Essendon, Victoria: Australian Churches of Christ Overseas Mission Board, 1990.

Filbeck, David. *The First Fifty Years: a Brief History of the Direct-support Missionary Movement*. Joplin, Missouri: College Press, 1980.

McLean, Archibald. *The History of the Foreign Christian Missionary Society*. New York; Chicago: Fleming H. Revell, 1919.

Priest, Doug. *Unto the Uttermost: Missions in the Christian Churches/ Churches of Christ*. Pasadena, California: William Carey Library, 1984.

Van Rheenen, Gailyn and Waldron, Bob. *The Status of Missions in Churches of Christ: a Nationwide Survey of Churches of Christ*. Abilene, Texas: ACU Press, 2002.

Website

Mission partners of Global Missions, Christian Church (Disciples of Christ). http://globalministries.org/eap/partners/; http://globalministries.org/sasia/partners/.

INDIA

They Went to India: Biographies of Missionaries of the Disciples of Christ. Indianapolis: Missionary Education Dept., United Christian Missionary Society, 1954

Bailey, J. C. *My Appointment with Destiny*. Fort Worth: Star Bible and Tract Corporation, 1975.

Website

Central India Christian Mission. http://indiamission.org/.

CHINA

Osgood, Elliot I. and Marx, Edwin. *The China Christian Mission: Completing Fifty Years of Service*. Indianapolis: United Christian Missionary Society, 1935.

TIBET

Dittemore, Isabel Maxey. *He Leadeth Me: Forty Years in Asia*. Joplin, MO: College Press, 1979.

Wissing, Douglas A. *Pioneer in Tibet: The Life and Perils of Dr. Albert Shelton*. New York: Palgrave Macmillan, 2004.

Zhao, Aidong, and Zhu, Xiaoling. *Far, Far Away in Remote Eastern Tibet: The Story of the American Doctor Albert Shelton and His Colleagues from the Disciples of Christ, 1903-1950*. St Louis: Lucas Park Books, 2014.

JAPAN

Miller, Bonnie. *Messengers of the Risen Son in the Land of the Rising Sun: Single Women Missionaries in Japan*. Abilene, Texas: Leafwood Publishers, 2008.

KOREA

Chae, Yoon Kwon. *A Short History of Korean Christian Churches and Churches of Christ*. Seoul, Korea: Yoon Kwon Chae. 2003.

PHILIPPINES

The Centennial Book of the Churches of Christ in the Philippines, 1901-2001. Manila, Philippines: Centennial Book of the Churches of Christ in the Philippines, 2002.

BURMA

Morse, Eugene. *Exodus to a Hidden Valley*. New York: Reader's Digest Press: 1974.

The Carribean and Latin America

T he Stone-Campbell movement came early to the English-speaking Caribbean since the third mission of the American Christian Missionary Society was in Jamaica. Missions were established later in the Spanish and Portuguese speaking areas of the Caribbean, Mexico, and Central and South America. In recent years numerical growth has accelerated in those areas.

JAMAICA

In 1858, the American Christian Missionary Society began support of the work of Julius Oliver Beardslee (1814–1879) a former Congregational minister in Jamaica. During his six years of work, supported by both the ACMS and British Churches of Christ, eighteen mission stations were established with 721 members. However, when the Christian Woman's Board of Missions sent William H. (1842–1938) and Martha Jane Williams to take over the mission in 1876, they only found five small churches. Later the leadership of W.K. and Anne Azbill helped stabilize the mission and led to growth, so that by 1926 there were twenty-five churches with 3,606 members, several schools, and twenty-three Jamaican pastors. In 1929 the Jamaican Association of Christian Churches began, led primarily by local leaders, so that when the missionaries were forced to leave during the Great Depression, the churches continued. The Association supported the ecumenical United Theological College of the West Indies and was also one of the earliest members of the World Council of Churches. Later known as the Synod of

135

Disciples of Christ in Jamaica, the association churches entered the United Church of Jamaica and the Cayman Islands in 1992.

Christian Women's Board of Mission

PUERTO RICO

In 1899 the American Christian Missionary Society sent J. A. Erwin to San Juan. William M. Taylor soon arrived and began the first church in Bayamon. Soon the Christian Woman's Board of Missions began orphanages whose schools had great influence. Vere C. (1978–1966) and Mayme (1882–1956) Carpenter began a thirty-eight year mission in 1906. These missionaries and others worked ecumenically by joining in the establishment of the joint Protestant Seminario Evangelico de Puerto Rico. Puerto Rican leadership of the missions increased through the appointment in 1922 of ordained ministers Augusto Cotto Reyes and Juan B. Ortiz to the mission board.

A significant event was the Revival of 1933 that began with prayer meetings where some experienced speaking in tongues. This led to evangelism and significant growth in the churches, from 1780 members in the churches in 1932 to over 5000 by 1947. It also led to conflict between Puerto Ricans and the United Christian Missionary Society missionaries. By 1965, the last missionary left and in 1967 the autonomous Convention of Christian Churches (Disciples of Christ) was formed, restructured as the Christian

Church (Disciples of Christ) in Puerto Rico in 1984, today with 104 congregations and over 22,000 members.

American Churches of Christ came to Puerto Rico through the work of Byrl Brockman, Clark Hannah, and Joe McKissick in the early 1950s. Other missionaries followed resulting in 32 churches with 1160 adherents today. Christian Churches/ Churches of Christ entered in 1954 through the mission of Gordon and Vivian Thompson. Today they have ten churches.

CUBA

In 1899, the Foreign Christian Missionary Society sent Lowell (1861–1949) and Clara (1869–1929) McPherson and Melvin (1868–1929) and Sue Menges to Havana, but closed the mission in 1907. A second mission station in Matanzas continued until 1917, led by Cubans Jacobo Gonzalez and Julio Fuentes. Beginning in the 1970s the Christian Church (Disciples of Christ) began a relationship with the Christian Pentecostal Church of Cuba.

U.S. Churches of Christ came to Cuba when Jose Ricardo Jimenez (1900–1974) returned to his homeland from Florida.

Juan Monroy

Through work begun by him and by Ernesto Estevez, by 1959 there were 161 churches with 5000 members. Due to the difficulties under Communist rule, by the 1980s there were only fifteen churches with 400 members. Beginning in the late 1980s several from Churches of Christ came on short-term missions, including Spanish evangelist Juan Antonio Monroy. Organizations like Healing Hands International have provided significant relief aid to Cuba, creating positive relations between the government and Churches of Christ. Today there are 120 churches with 5000 members.

OTHER CARIBBEAN COUNTRIES

There are several Stone-Campbell churches in Haiti, and at least one congregation in Anguilla, Antigua and Barbuda, Aruba, the Bahamas, Barbados, Bermuda, the British Virgin Islands, the Cayman Islands, Dominica, the Dominican Republic, French Guiana, Grenada, Guadeloupe, the Netherland Antilles, Saint Kitts and Nevis, Saint Lucia, Saint Martin, Saint Vincent and the Grenadines, Trinidad and Tobago, and the Turks and Caicos Islands.

MEXICO

The Christian Woman's Board of Missions began the support of the work of Merritt L. Hoblit in Cuidad Juarez, Mexico in 1895. Others, like Bertha Mason, joined that mission that soon moved to Monterrey. By 1900 the first church was formed with Mexican leadership. Thomas Westrop (1837–1909) and his wife Francesca Barocio (1853–1910) translated hymns into Spanish, began schools, and expanded the mission northward. During the Mexican Revolution (1910–1917), American missionaries fled Mexico, leaving evangelists like Felipe Jimenez to lead the Monterrey churches. The CWBM moved their mission to central Mexico by 1919, moving toward indigenization of the work. By the 1960s Mexican leaders developed a "Revolutionary Plan for Evangelism, resulting in 290 baptisms and a new church in Mexico City. In 1963, the churches formed the Association of Evangelical Christian Churches (Disciples of Christ). Unfortunately, a dispute over property led by

Mexico and Central America

1993 to two groups of Stone-Campbell Christians from this mission heritage, the Fellowship of Christian Churches (Disciples of Christ) and the Alliance of Evangelical Christian Churches (Disciples of Christ).

When the CWBM moved their mission to central Mexico in 1919, Enrique Westrup and others continued the Monterrey work as a direct support mission. Later Antonio Medina became a direct support missionary, planting more than a dozen churches. Schools like the Colegio Biblico, founded by Harlan and Francis Cary in 1944, and the Mexican Bible Seminary, founded by Gerald and Geneva Bowlin in 1950, were important in training Mexican ministers. Today churches in Mexico associated with Christian Churches and Churches of Christ number 260 with 14,300 adherents.

Churches of Christ first entered Mexico through three attempts at establishing Christian colonies of immigrants from the United States between 1897 and 1911. However, successful evangelism began in 1932 when Pedro Rivas returned to Mexico from study at Freed-Hardeman College in Tennessee. Settling in Torreon, he and others started a school of preaching as well as planting churches. Later another school was established at Monterrey. Today there are over 400 Churches of Christ with over 25,000 members in Mexico.

CENTRAL AMERICA

The Jerry Hill, Carl James, Floyd Hill, and Hignacio Huerto families from American Churches of Christ entered Guatemala in 1959. They soon planted five churches, preached on the radio, began a newspaper, and cultivated local church leadership. Other families from the United States joined them in 1970 to build indigenous churches.

One significant event coming from that mission was the first Pan American Lectureship, held in Guatemala City in 1963. The annual lectureship, held in various Central American cities, encouraged the planting of churches in Panama in 1963, El Salvador in 1965, Costa Rica in 1967, Nicaragua in 1968, Honduras in 1969, and Belize in 1971. It also led to medical work like that sponsored by Predisan in Honduras, founded by Dr. Robert and Doris Clark in 1986. As a result of five decades of evangelism there are almost 1300 congregations of Churches of Christ with over 130,000 adherents in Central America.

The Division of Overseas Ministries of the Christian Church (Disciples of Christ) sent two professors, Carmelo Alvarez and Raquel Rodriguez, to teach in the Latin America Biblical Seminary in San Jose, Costa Rica in 1975. Disciples have partnered with several churches in Central America, notably to assist in war-torn El Salvador in the 1980s and 1990s.

In the 1990s, Timothy Peppers of the Goldsboro-Raleigh District of the Church of Christ, Disciples of Christ International began work in Panama. In 2004 Bishop Chester L. Aycock officially welcomed seven Panamanian churches with 800 members into the Church of Christ, Disciples of Christ International.

ARGENTINA

Under the sponsorship of the Christian Woman's Board of Missions, Willis (1870–1957) and Lulu (d. 1927) Burner came to Belgrano near Buenos Aires in 1906. Four other missionaries soon joined

Jorgelina Lozada

them, but found it difficult to establish churches, with only two with 139 members by the late 1920s. By 1929, Argentine leaders were included in the Central Council of Disciple Churches that soon held an annual convention. In the 1940s the United Christian Missionary Society sent twelve additional missionaries, including T.J. (1919–2012) and Virginia (1918–2002) Liggett who worked with Argentine Feliciano Sarli in Resistencia. Jorgelina Lozada (1906–1995) served as pastor of the Villa Mitre Christian Church and served ecumenically as a delegate to the 1938 World Mission Conference in Madras, India, the 1950 World Sunday School Convention, the 1952 International Missionary Council, and the 1954 General Assembly of the World Council of Churches in Evanston, Illinois, United States.

In 1959 the church became the autonomous Evangelical Church of the Disciples of Christ in Argentina. Church members suffered during the "Dirty War" of 1976–1983 in Argentina. Today the body numbers five congregations and 640 members.

Silvero Ojeda, a former Catholic priest, began work supported by Churches of Christ in 1957. Through the years at least twenty-eight missionaries have worked in Argentina, resulting in fifteen congregations with over 500 members. Christian Churches/ Churches of Christ also have a mission in Argentina.

PARAGUAY

In 1918, the Christian Woman's Board of Mission began a work in Asuncion, Paraguay, led by C. Manly (1884–1976) and Selah (1886–1970) Morton. In 1919, they founded the Colegio International, a coeducational boarding school. By 1928, there was a church at the school, but opposition from some Catholic leaders, the Chaco War, and the Great Depression all hindered church building. The best known ministry growing from the mission was the establishment of a leper colony in 1934 by Dr. John Hay (1863–1943) and Malcolm Norment (1890–1969), supported by the United Christian Missionary Society. Through the 1950s and 1960s more church planting took place, as the churches indigenized as the Christian Church, Disciples of Christ in Paraguay. In spite of difficult political situations, those churches today number over a dozen with 3600 adherents.

Luis Ramirez, beginning in 1976, and the Forest McDonald family from 1981–1984, served as missionaries from U.S. Churches of Christ in Paraguay. In 2003 the mission organization Continent of Great Cities sent a team to Asuncion who has since planted three congregations.

South America

BRAZIL

In 1948, Lloyd David Sanders, a recent graduate of Johnson Bible College and Phillips University, and his wife Ruth came to Brazil as missionaries. Settling in the Goias area, they began to plant churches. When the new capital of Brazil, Brasilia, began in 1960, the Sanders secured one of the first church sites. As a result of their more than seventy years of work, there are over 300 churches in Goias and the Federal District,

Lloyd David Sanders

led by Brazilian ministers. More than thirty other direct support missionaries associated with Christian Churches/Churches of Christ have worked in Brazil. The vast majority of churches today have Brazilian pastors who are organized as the Ministerial Council of the Churches of Christ in Brazil. That council organized the 2012 Global Gathering of the World Convention of Churches of Christ in Goiania, the first Gathering to be held in the Global South, with an attendance of almost 4000. Today these Brazilian Christian Churches number 440 churches with a membership of over 90,000. The Brazilian churches send out and support Brazilian missionaries in Mozambique, Angola, Guinea-Bissau, Mexico, Portugal, the United States, and India. In 2011 Brazilian Churches partnered with Korean churches to plant the Korean speaking Bom Retiro church near São Paulo.

American Churches of Christ first came to Brazil through the work of three missionary couples that settled in Mata Grande in the late 1920s. With Brazilian workers, they planted several churches in Ceara, Rio Grande do Norte, Paraiba, and elsewhere. However the missionaries and a majority of churches joined the Assembly of God in 1935.

Churches of Christ returned in 1956 through the work of Arlie and Alma Smith in São Paulo. By 1961, fourteen families joined

143

them, planting a dozen churches and preaching on several radio stations. From 1967 to 1970 over one hundred missionaries came to Belo Horizonte, planting churches there and eventually in Recife, Brasilia, Salvador, and other cities, so that today there are around 160 churches with 22,000 members.

Since the 1960s the Christian Church (Disciples of Christ) has sent fraternal workers to minister in three Brazilian churches that are ecumenical partners: the United Presbyterian Church of Brazil, the Association of the Methodist Church in Brazil, and the Evangelical Congregational Church of Brazil.

OTHER SOUTH AMERICAN COUNTRIES

Beginning in the late 1940s American Disciples began a relationship with the Evangelical Pentecostal Union of Venezuela. Beginning in 1963 missionaries Juan Marcos and Flor Rivera along with many Disciple fraternal workers from the United States and Puerto Rico cemented that ecumenical relationship. Churches of Christ entered Venezuela through the work of Atilo Pinto and Clifford Tucker in Caracas. Bob Brown provided leadership for the churches from 1977 to 1995, though most evangelists today are Venezuelan.

In 1949, Bertrand Smith began a direct support mission to Valparaiso, Chile. Other missionaries from Christian Churches/ Churches of Christ followed in the 1960s and 1970s, planting churches in Concepcion and Santiago. Christian Missionary Fellowship sent a team to Chile in 1988. Churches of Christ entered Chile in 1961 through the mission of Vernon Hawkins and Phil Morgan. In 1981 the Tom Hook family arrived and later planted a church in Vina del Mar.

Other missions from American Churches of Christ include that of D. H. Hadwin (1906–1996) in Montevideo, Uruguay beginning in 1952. Other workers followed in the 1970s to through the 1990s. N.E. Sewell spent ten years in Ecuador beginning in 1967. Jim Lanier worked in Surinam from 1971–1975. Glen and Janice Kramar brought Churches of Christ to Lima, Peru in 1963. In 1973, missionaries from Peru and Argentina first came to Bolivia, and a mission team arrived in 1983. In the 1960s Jerry Browning and Delbert Bradley worked in Guyana. Bernie Mullins and others came in 1985 to reestablish that work. In Colombia, Jaime Solar and Charles F. Krull arrived in 1965, but violence forced American missionaries to leave by 1987. The churches in Colombia continue to thrive with local leaders.

Continent of Great Cities (now Great Cities Missions) from Churches of Christ sent mission teams to Montevideo, Uruguay in 1992, Santiago, Chile in 1999, Bogotá, Columbia in 2003, Cusco, Peru in 2009, and La Paz, Bolivia in 2013.

Stone-Campbell churches are growing in Latin America, particularly in urban areas. As in other parts of the world, most of what began as "mission" churches are now led by indigenous ministers and leaders. Those Christians display a vibrant, emotional, and dedicated faith, shown in their efforts to plant other churches locally and worldwide.

QUESTIONS FOR DISCUSSION

1. In many of these countries our churches supported a union college or seminary with other denominations instead of beginning their own schools. Why was this done? What is the best approach, union schools or those associated only with our own churches?

2. Latin America was one of the first places to which American churches sent large mission teams instead of a few individuals or families. What are the advantages of large teams? Disadvantages?

3. Stone-Campbell churches in Latin America are sending missionaries to several countries. Where are they going? Why those places? What does this say about missions and evangelism worldwide?

4.   What did you find most surprising or significant in this chapter?

For Further Reading

Foster, Douglas A., Newell Williams, Paul M. Blowers, and Anthony L. Dunnavant, eds. *The Encyclopedia of the Stone-Campbell Movement*. Grand Rapids, Michigan: Eerdmans, 2004. See articles Jamaica, the Movement in; Latin America and Caribbean, Missions in; Puerto Rico, the Movement in.

Williams, Newell, Douglas Foster, and Paul Blowers. *The Stone-Campbell Movement: A Global History*. St. Louis, Missouri: Chalice 2013. See pages 142–150, 285–310.

Website

Global Ministries Christian Church (Disciples of Christ). http://globalministries.org/lac/partners/.

Jamaica

Nelson, Robert Gilbert. *Disciples of Christ in Jamaica, 1858–1958; a Centennial of Missions in the "Gem of the Caribbean."* St. Louis, Bethany Press, 1958.

Puerto Rico

Carpenter, Vere Clifton. *Puerto Rican Disciples: a personal narrative of fifty years with Christ in the island of enchantment*. Tampa, Florida: Christian Press, 1960.

Morton, Clement Manly. *Kingdom Building in Puerto Rico: a Story of Fifty Years of Christian Service*. Indianapolis: United Christian Missionary Society, 1949.

Vargas, Joaquin. *Los Discipulos de Cristo en Puerto Rico: Albores, Crecimiento y Madurez de un Peregrinar de Fe, Constancia y Esperanze, 1899–1987*. Puerto Rico: Iglesia Cristiana (Discipulos de Cristo) en Puerto Rico, 1988.

Mexico

Irelan, Elam C. *Fifty Years with our Mexican Neighbors*. Saint Louis: The Bethany Press, 1944.

ARGENTINA

Montgomery, J. Dexter. *Disciples of Christ in Argentina, 1906–1956; a History of the First Fifty Years of Mission Work*. St. Louis, Bethany Press, 1956.

PARAGUAY

Mills, Elizabeth Eastman. *Adventuring With Christ in Paraguay: Fifty Years of Service, 1920–1970*. Rosemead, California: Author, 1973.

BRAZIL

Gilpatrick, Teston. *Lessons on Missions from 20 Years in Sao Paulo: an Evaluation of the Impact of the Sao Paulo Mission Team on the Churches of Christ in Sao Paulo, Brazil, From 1961 to 1981*. Winona, Mississippi: J.C. Choate Publications, 1982.

Africa, the New Center of Christianity

The Stone-Campbell Movement came to Africa as early as 1854 with the brief work of Alexander Cross in Liberia, sponsored by the American Christian Missionary Society. Thus for over 260 years through the work of missionaries from around the world and the work and leadership of indigenous ministers, the movement has grown in Africa. Today there are more adherents (members and children) in the Stone-Campbell churches in Africa than on any continent, including North America, the birthplace of the movement. Africa has truly become the new center of Christianity and of the Stone-Campbell Movement.

SOUTHERN AFRICA

The first lasting mission to Africa came from efforts of the British Commonwealth stream of the movement. Henry Elliott Tickle from the Foreign Missionary Committee of the British Churches of Christ emigrated from England to South Africa in 1892. He found other immigrants from the movement and urged them to form local congregations. The Foreign Missionary Committee sent R. K. Francis in 1902 who alongside others established churches leading to the first annual conference of the churches in Johannesburg in 1905.

In 1906 the church at Roodeport began to work among the black population, with Agrippa Mzozoiyana and George Khosa leading the work. By the 1920s the white churches were shrinking while the number of black and colored members was increasing.

Thomas Kalane studied at Wilberforce University in the United States and was sent by the Tabernacle Christian Church in Columbus, Indiana to be a missionary to South Africa in 1921. He was spectacularly successful in his work in Kimberly, with over 3000 conversions, but personal and political controversies led to his being deported to his native Mozambique.

Charles Buttz Titus along with Carl and Clara Lewis led the Kimberly mission in the 1920s forming the African Christian Missionary Society to help gain financial support from the United States. By the end of the 1920s it had twenty mission stations, sixty-three outstations, and over twenty indigenous missionaries. In 1925, the Thomas Evangelistic Mission, supported financially by Dallas Businessman M.H. Thomas, led to thousands being baptized and many new churches. The Great Depression and some internal controversy led to the mission's closure by 1930, and most missionaries returned home. By then, however, there were nine white congregations with almost 800 total members and many black and colored churches with a combined membership of several thousand, led by indigenous leaders like Simon Sibenya, T.D. Mathibe, and George Khosa.

Sabina Sibenya

From America in 1945, the United Christian Missionary Society sent Basil F. and Margaret Holt as a mission leaders and organizers. The Holts quickly organized the South African Association of the Disciples of Christ (Churches of Christ), worked toward ecumenical and interdenominational cooperation, began a newspaper for the association—*The South African Sentinel*—and worked toward racial reconciliation and justice.

In the early 1950s, Canadian missionaries William and Melba Rees began their work in Kimberly. They were soon joined by Max Ward and Gladys Randall from the United States. They organized churches, started a paper, and began a school to train black and colored evangelists, convinced that the churches needed to be led by indigenous ministers and should be self-governing and self-supporting. When the United Congregational Church of Southern Africa was formed in 1972, most of the churches in the South African Association of the Disciples of Christ (Churches of Christ) joined the united church.

In the late 1950s many missionaries from the American Christian Churches/Churches of Christ came to South Africa, including Al and Jean Zimmerman in Cape Town, and Stuart and Marilyn Cook in Johannesburg and later in Limpopo. Missionaries from American Churches of Christ such as John and Bessie Hardin, Guy and Jesse Caskey, Robert "Tex" (b. 1928) and Mary Jane Williams, Foy Short, and Eldred Echols (1920–2003), also came in the 1950s. They used Bible correspondence courses and radio broadcasts effectively in their ministry, and by the 1970s the ministry had shifted from direct church planting by missionaries to training indigenous evangelists through schools of preaching.

In South Africa in 2014, there were approximately 900 congregations with 85,000 adherents associated with Christian Churches/Churches of Christ and 500 congregations with 33,000 adherents associated with Churches of Christ. Churches of Christ operate African Christian College in Swaziland, and South African Bible College in Benoni near Johannesburg. The Common Global Missions Board of the Christian Church (Disciples of Christ) in the

United States and Canada maintains a partnership with the United Congregational Church of Southern Africa.

In 1975 South African Greg Woods from Churches of Christ began a congregation in Windhoek, Namibia. Patrick Selemela, Dean Troyer, and Mike Tanaro from Churches of Christ came to Botswana in 1974, eventually forming a church in Gaborone. Jerry and Edith Sullins started the Botswana School of Biblical Studies in 1988, but the school moved to Zambia in 1996. Work began in Lesotho as early as 1962 when George Raseleso returned home from South Africa. Several missionaries from American Churches of Christ have worked there, resulting in several congregations.

SOUTHERN RHODESIA (ZIMBABWE), NORTHERN RHODESIA (ZAMBIA), AND MALAWI

John Sherriff (1864–1935) from New Zealand was the most influential early missionary to Rhodesia. He arrived in South Africa in 1896 and settled in Bulawayo in Rhodesia in 1897. Some of his earliest converts were George McKenna, Agrippa Mzozoiyana, Charles Kakha, and George Khosa—who all became influential evangelists in Rhodesia and in South Africa. Later Sherriff returned briefly to New Zealand, recruited other missionaries, and convinced the Foreign Mission Council of the New Zealand Churches of Christ to support the mission. Upon his return to Rhodesia, he bought a large farm outside Bulawayo to train ministers. Later the headquarters of the mission was moved to Intini, then to Dadaya. The mission had its own paper, the *Foreign Mission News*, and eventually received support from churches in Canada, the United States, Australia, and New Zealand. By the late 1920s the mission had 22 churches with a membership of around 1,200, and 16 schools.

John Sherriff died in 1935, and the year before his death, Garfield (1908–2002) and Grace (1911–2001) Todd were sent to Rhodesia by the New Zealand Foreign Mission Union. They focused their efforts on education, doubling the enrollment in their schools between 1934 and 1946, resulting in trained local leaders for the churches. In 1953, Garfield Todd was elected Prime Minister

John Sherriff in South Africa

of Rhodesia. Ray Knapp and A. W. and C. M. Ladbrook gradually became leaders of the Dadaya Mission. Gradually through the 1960s and 1970s, indigenous leaders took over the work, leading to the establishment of the self-supporting and governing Associated Churches of Christ in Zimbabwe in 1973. Today those churches have over 80,000 adherents.

Dewitt and Dollie Garrett from North American Churches of Christ came to Salisbury, Rhodesia in 1931. In 1940, W. L. and Addie Brown also from North American Churches of Christ established the Nhowe mission that included a school and clinic. Later missionaries to Nhowe included Dr. Marjorie Sewell and Dr. Anne Stricklin. In 2014, adherents to these Churches of Christ in Zimbabwe numbered over 40,000. In 1956, John and Marjorie Pemberton from North American Christian Churches/Churches of Christ received responsibility for the Mashoko Mission from the Foreign Mission Union of the New Zealand Churches of Christ. This eventually grew into the Central Africa Mission, which in turn established ten other mission points. Adherents of Christian

Churches/Churches of Christ today in Zimbabwe number over 250,000.

In the 1910s, two converts of John Sherriff, Peter Masiya and Jack Mzilwa, began to evangelize in Northern Rhodesia (today Zambia). Two missionaries from North American Churches of Christ, W. N. and A'Delia Short, joined them in Sinde. Peter Masiya evangelized Kambole Mpatamatenga, who worked at the Kabanga mission, the Siamundele station, and later started a mission school in his house. Most significantly, he translated the New Testament into the Chitonga and Lozi languages. Several other missionaries from North American Churches of Christ came after the Great Depression, so that by 1948 they had established twenty-five schools with forty-two indigenous teachers and total enrollment of 2,133. The work continued to grow after the establishment of the Republic of Zambia in 1964. In 2014 there were over 1300 congregations with over 80,000 adherents.

The work of John Sherriff also led to the planting churches in Nyasaland (today Malawi). His convert Ellerton Kundago returned to Nyasaland from working in Bulawayo and soon converted others and began a church. George Hubert Hollis and George Hills arrived from Cape Town in 1909, joined by Mary Banister and Henry and Etta Philpott from Britain in 1913 (supported by the British Foreign Missions Committee). These missionaries focused on training and encouraging indigenous ministers who made extensive evangelistic journeys. Unfortunately, the colonial government associated Churches of Christ with an uprising against white plantation owners in 1915. As a result, the missionaries were banned and not allowed to return until 1927.

In 1928, Mary Bannister, one of the missionaries who had been expelled, returned to Nyasaland. The next year the British Foreign Missions Committee purchased a mission station at Gowa from the Baptists. Soon other missionaries arrived, with Ernest Gray providing leadership in education. By 1960, the mission consisted of thirty-four churches with total membership of four thousand, fourteen African ministers, and thirty-three schools with enrollment of over 3,800. After independence in 1964, the missions united into the Churches of Christ in Malawi, moving their headquarters from Gowa to Lilongwe in 2000. Today they have 61 churches and 50,000 adherents.

North American Churches of Christ came to northern Nyasaland in the 1950s through the work of indigenous evangelists Ahaziah Apollo Ngwira, Timothy Zimba, and Godwin Mukwakwa. American missionaries Andrew and Claudine Connally, James and Clydene Judd, and Doyle and Louis Gilliam came in 1957 to organize the Lubagha Mission. Other work was established in central Malawi so that by 2014 there were 4100 congregations with over 225,000 adherents associated with American Churches of Christ. In the 1950s missionaries Paul and Wilma Nichols from American non-institutional Churches of Christ arrived in Nyasaland. As a result of their work and that of other missionaries and indigenous evangelists, over 900 churches with 75,000 adherents are in Malawi today.

The Congo

Over one million members of the Eglise du Christ au Congo trace their roots to the work of Ellsworth E. Farris (1874–1953) who was sent by the Foreign Christian Missionary Society of the United States to the Congo in 1897. He was soon joined by Dr. Royal (1874–1966) and Eva (1977–1951) Dye. Royal opened a clinic at the Bolenge mission station and Eva worked on Bible translation. The Disciples of Christ Congo Mission was dedicated to developing indigenous leaders. One of those early leaders was Mark Njoji who studied at Eureka College in the United States. The mission was boosted in 1909 when churches in the Pacific Northwest of the United States raised funds for a steamship, the *S. S. Oregon* that would travel the Congo River as a "gospel boat." This led to an additional six mission stations by 1925 with 689 Congolese workers in 350 outstations. In 1928 the Institut Chretien Conglais was established, offering a three-year course in many subjects including training for ministry.

The church continued to grow throughout the 1940s and 1950s, supported by the United Christian Missionary Society of the North

The Oregon Congo Boat

American Disciples. By the time the Congo gained independence in 1960, the Congolese church had also begun to be self-supporting and self-governing. Under the leadership of Itofo Jean Bokeleale, the church continued its long-standing commitment to ecumenism by joining a union of sixty-two church bodies in 1970 to form the *Eglise du Christ au Congo* with the churches with roots from the Disciples of Christ Congo Mission known as the Community of Disciples of Christ.

In the late 1970s Angolan refugees who had settled in the Democratic Republic of the Congo, came into contact with the Stone-Campbell Movement, and later established churches upon their return to Angola. Missionaries from Brazil were working there beginning in the 1980s. Today those churches have over 28,000 adherents. Missionaries from the Community of Disciples of Christ from the Democratic Republic of the Congo planted churches in the Republic of the Congo (Congo-Brazzaville) in 1995, resulting in the Church of the Disciples of Christ of the Congo with two thousand members today.

There are also a few Churches of Christ in Chad due to Chadians receiving Bible correspondence courses, and then planting churches.

EAST AFRICA

Missionaries from North American Churches of Christ began to plant churches in East Africa after World War II. Eldred Echols and Guy Caskey (1917–2003) moved from South Africa to Tanganyika (Tanzania) in 1952, establishing the Tanganyika Bible School near Chimala to train African evangelists in 1956. That school closed in 1971 but was replaced by the Chimala School of Preaching in 1987. In 1964, Andrew (1931–1992) and Claudine Connally raised the funds for a clinic that eventually became Chimala Hospital. Other missionaries opened new work in Tanzania so that today there are over 165 churches and 12,000 adherents.

In Ethiopia, Carl Thompson and Bob Gowen came from North American Churches of Christ to Addis Ababa in 1960. Soon they opened a school for the deaf. Ato Shongeh Sabaybo had begun his own evangelistic work in the Sidamo Province and later joined with the missionaries from North American Churches of Christ. Behailu Abebe administered relief assistance during the Ethiopian famine of 1984–1987. Because of the work of these and other Ethiopia leaders, by 2014 there were 670 churches with over 60,000 adherents associated with North American Churches of Christ.

The Christian Missionary Fellowship of North American Christian Churches/Churches of Christ sent Mont and Elaine Smith to Ethiopia in 1963. Other missionaries, including Doug Priest, Jr. (b. 1952) joined their efforts. They left in 1977 due to the Marxist revolution, but in 1992 a new group of missionaries from the Christian Missionary Fellowship entered the country. Today those churches number one hundred and ten with over 40,000 adherents.

The 1500 congregations and over 40,000 adherents of Churches of Christ in Kenya trace their origin to the arrival of Van and Jean Tate, and Ted and Martha Ogle in Nairobi in 1965. They were joined in the early 1970s by several other couples from North American Churches of Christ. Later this mission established two schools, the Nairobi Great Commission School in 1990 and the Kenya Christian Industrial Training Institute in 1991. Also arriving in Nairobi in 1965 were Howard and Jane Crowl from North American Christian Churches/Churches of Christ. Other missionaries joined them and Christian Missionary Fellowship continued to support these missionaries and local leaders in the tasks of developing African leaders, church planting, and medical and orphan care. In 2014 there are 313 churches and over 19,000 adherents of these churches.

Stone-Campbell churches in Mozambique began through the work of Dias Bento Feliciano, who had joined Churches of Christ while living in Nyasaland in 1959. Returning home, he later worked with Carlos Esteves and other missionaries from Portugal and Brazil. In 1992 missionaries arrived from North American Christian Churches/Churches of Christ to lead the Maputo Biblical and Theological Seminary to train local evangelists. Today there are over 30,000 adherents in Stone-Campbell churches in Mozambique.

Other nations in East Africa—Uganda, Rwanda, Madagascar, Mauritius, Morocco, the Seychelles, Sudan, and South Sudan—all have small but growing numbers of Christians from the Stone-Campbell Movement.

West Africa

The Stone-Campbell Movement came to Nigeria and West Africa through an indigenous mission work led by Coolidge Akpan Okon Essien (1915–1960). He and other Nigerian evangelists led forty-nine churches and over 10,000 members, before he enrolled in 1948 in a Bible correspondence course offered by the Lawrence Avenue Church of Christ in Nashville, Tennessee. As a result of that course, these churches were connected with North American Churches of Christ who began to send missionaries to Nigeria in 1952. They established preacher training schools and a system of village schools enrolling over 2,500 students by 1959. In 1964 Dr. Henry (1926–2010) and Grace (1924–2013) Farrar arrived and soon founded Nigerian Christian Hospital.

Africans Claiming Africa (2008)

The Nigerian Civil War (1967–1970) caused great loss of life and property for the churches. Most American missionaries left Nigeria, some planting churches in nearby Cameroon. After the war, Dr. Farrar reopened the hospital; Upkom Bible College grew into Nigerian Christian Bible College, and leadership of churches and other institutions passed into Nigerian hands. By 2014, there were over 3000 congregations and almost 300,000 adherents of Churches of Christ and thirty churches with over 6,000 adherents of Christian Churches/Churches of Christ.

In Ghana, John Gaidoo (d. 1961) a major in the Salvation Army, also came into Churches of Christ through a Bible correspondence course. He established several congregations near Accra before missionaries Jerry Reynolds and Dewayne Davenport came to Kumasi in 1961. Working with Samuel Buahin Obeng and other evangelists, they founded Ghana Bible College there in 1962. Heritage Christian College in Accra followed in 1982. Since the mid 1960s Ghanaians have led churches and institutions—including the Village of Hope orphanage, school, and medical clinic. In

2014 their churches numbered over 1100 with over 80,000 adherents. Ghanaian evangelists also planted churches in Togo, Cote d'Ivorie, Burkina Faso, Benin, the Gambia, Libya, Senegal, Mali, Gabon, Central African Republic, Mauritania, and Equatorial Guinea.

In August 1963 the first missionaries from Christian Churches/ Churches of Christ came to Ghana, establishing Ghana Christian College in 1966. Those churches organized into the fellowship of Christian Churches in 2011 with over two hundred churches.

A partnership between Bishop Chester Aycock of the Church of Christ, Disciples of Christ, and Ghanaian minister Ebenezer Sefah of the Refreshing Hour Churches has led to one hundred and fifty churches with over ten thousand members in Ghana associated with the Goldsboro-Raleigh Assembly of the Church of Christ, Disciples of Christ.

In West Africa, small numbers of Stone-Campbell churches are also found in Guinea-Bissau, Mali, Senegal, Niger, Sierra Leone, and Liberia.

Pan-African Leadership

As noted above, several Stone-Campbell churches in Africa have developed regional or national leadership bodies. Leaders from the movement from many countries in Africa have met regularly for fellowship and to share evangelistic strategy. For example, for over thirty years there has been an annual meeting called the Southern Africa International Lectureship. The Africans Claiming Africa for Christ conference has met every four years since 1992, in Kenya, Zimbabwe, South Africa, Ghana, Nigeria, and Zambia, drawing church leaders from throughout the continent. A Global Gathering of the World Convention was planned for Zimbabwe for 2012, but was moved to Brazil due to the collapse of the Zimbabwean economy. However, B. J. Mpofu of Zimbabwe served as President of the World Convention from 2008 to 2012. Perhaps in the future locally, nationally, and in all of Africa, leaders from Stone-Campbell churches associated with all the American streams can work together in visible ways to continue spreading the gospel throughout Africa.

Questions for Discussion

1. Why did many of the earliest missionaries to Africa come from Britain and Commonwealth countries instead of from the United States?

2. What countries in Africa have the largest numbers of Christians from the Stone-Campbell churches? Why do you think the numbers are greater in those countries?

3. Why have these churches grown so rapidly in Africa compared with most of the rest of the world?

4. What have been the roles of schools and hospitals in the evangelization of Africa? Why have these been so important?

5. In the last fifty years, there has been a shifted from direct church planting by missionaries from outside Africa to training indigenous evangelists. Is this a healthy shift? Why or why not?

For Further Reading

Foster, Douglas A., Newell Williams, Paul M. Blowers, and Anthony L. Dunnavant, eds. *The Encyclopedia of the Stone-Campbell Movement*. Grand Rapids, Michigan: Eerdmans, 2004. See article Africa, Missions in.

Williams, Newell, Douglas Foster, and Paul Blowers. *The Stone-Campbell Movement: A Global History*. St. Louis, Missouri: Chalice 2013. See pages 133–142, 311–343.

Website
Global Ministries (Christian Church (Disciples of Christ). http://globalministries.org/africa/partners/.

Casey, Michael. *The Rhetoric of Sir Garfield Todd: Christian Imagination and the Dream of an African Democracy*. Waco, Texas: Baylor University Press, 2007.

Dye, Polly C. and Margaret Heppe. *In His Glad Service: the Story of Royal J. and Eva Dye.* Eugene, Oregon: Northwest Christian College, 1975.

Granberg, Stanley E. *100 Years of African Missions: Essays in Honor of Wendell Broom.* Abilene: ACU Press, 2001.

Johnson, Gene E. *Congo Centennial: The Second Fifty Years.* Galesburg, Ill.: First Christian Church, 1999

Priest, Doug. *Doing Theology with the Maasai,* Pasadena, California: William Carey Library, 1990.

Randall, Max Ward. *We Would Do It Again: Epitome of Evangelism Recounted and Portrayed on the Field of the Churches of Christ Mission, Inc., in the Land of South Africa.* Joliet: Mission Services, 1965.

A Global Movement Faces the Future

In two centuries the Stone-Campbell Movement has grown from a handful of leaders in the United States and Britain to a worldwide movement of over ten million in 199 countries. How did that happen? One clear answer is evangelism. The usual pattern was for countries to send out missionaries who would evangelize, then train local leaders, eventually leading to indigenous churches independent of but still in fellowship with the churches of the sending country. Today mission is seen primarily as a partnership between sending and receiving churches. Few missionaries see themselves as "running a mission" but rather as assisting local leaders in spreading the Good News through proclamation, education, medical assistance, agricultural instruction, and economic justice. Also today many countries are both "receiving" and "sending" nations, with Koreans sending missionaries to Brazil, Brazilians to Mozambique, Indians to China, and many African countries to the United States.

WHERE ARE THESE STONE-CAMPBELL CHURCHES?

Space would not allow for the story of all our churches to be told in a brief book. The numbers of adherents below give some idea of where these churches are most numerous. Keep in mind that it is difficult to get accurate numbers, particularly in Asia and Africa. For example there may be well over a million adherents in India alone. Indeed the numbers below from the *World Christian Database* (2010) sometimes differ from our best estimates given in the other chapters in this book.

Congo DR	1,052,000	South Africa	83,400
Ghana	700,000	Australia	68,800
Zimbabwe	360,500	Brazil	63,000
Philippines	324,000	Mexico	58,900
Malawi	175,900	Central African Republic	55,200
Nigeria	171,800	Guatemala	46,100
Zambia	140,400	Papua New Guinea	35,300
Kenya	114,700	India	34,500
Ethiopia	100,000	Angola	26,200
South Korea	84,400		

Or by continent:

North America	3,254,109	Latin America	367,290
Africa	3,064,860	Oceania/Australia	124,120
Asia/Middle East	490,370	Europe	72,770

Some countries with nationally organized work cooperate through the Disciples Ecumenical Consultative Council. The World Convention of Churches of Christ is a global fellowship that exists to cooperate with Christians everywhere toward the unity of the Church by building fellowship, understanding, and common purpose within the Stone-Campbell Movement's global family. World Convention sponsors a Global Gathering for the Movement every four years. Beginning in Goiania, Brazil in 2012 and New Delhi, India in 2017, the gatherings increasingly reflect the realities of the shift of the center of population of Christianity to the global south.

A COMMON IDENTITY
In these chapters we have briefly told the story of the Stone-Campbell Movement in all its richness and diversity. There is great diversity among these churches in organization, worship, and theology. In

Peter Ainslie and Others

many countries the churches have no formal organization beyond the local congregation, while in others there are state or national conventions, national ministerial councils, and national organizations including some with a modified episcopacy. Worship in some churches is orderly and sedate. In others it is enthusiastic and charismatic. Some are involved in ecumenical organizations while others still tend toward an exclusive sectarian. These churches are not all alike.

Yet there is a common Stone-Campbell identity that transcends these differences. Today in any Christian World Communion there is great diversity in belief and practice. There are also many features of each family that are shared by the whole church of Jesus Christ. What follows is an attempt to create an overarching but simple picture of who these churches are as part of the whole church.[1]

---

[1] These characteristics are adapted from a statement prepared by Lorraine & Lyndsay Jacobs, former General Secretaries of the World Convention of Churches of Christ.

1. A CONCERN FOR CHRISTIAN UNITY.

In the 1808 *Declaration and Address,* Thomas Campbell wrote that the "Church of Christ on earth is essentially, intentionally and constitutionally one." Barton Stone, said, "Let the Unity of Christians be our polar star." The 'Christian' movement was a movement for unity within the fragmented and often hostile and competitive church environment of that time. Today there are different understandings of how Christian unity might be understood and achieved ranging from commitment to the ecumenical movement, with some involved in dialogue and with other church families, through a belief that there is already an underlying God-given unity despite apparent division, to those who feel that they have discovered what the church should be like and that unity will come through others recognizing this and joining with them. The Stone-Campbell movement is convinced that unity is both the gift of God and the calling of all Christians.

2. A COMMITMENT TO EVANGELISM AND MISSION.

Unity was never an end in itself, but was always connected with evangelism since Jesus himself connected them in his prayer that "all might be one... so that the world might believe" (see John 17:20–23). This book has told a few of the countless stories of evangelism and mission that has made this a worldwide movement.

3. AN EMPHASIS ON SCRIPTURE.

This movement began as one of several "Back to the Bible" movements. Early leaders believed that unity could be achieved by restoring to the New Testament Church things that it had lost, thus stripping away the accumulation of traditions that had brought about division. Today many still like to be referred to as the 'Restoration Movement'; others believe there are difficulties in accepting that the New Testament provides a clear unified model for the church and believe that the church must also be open to God's present word measured against the biblical revelation. But in spite of differences in interpretation, all seek renewal of the church and the world on biblical principles.

4. A CALL TO PEACE AND JUSTICE.

Unity, evangelism, and renewal were all for the purpose of participating in God's reign of peace and justice. Stone-Campbell churches have pursued peace and justice in various ways—through caring for the sick, orphans, refugees and others in need through church action and the establishment of compassion ministries. Some have been pacifists, believing that is the best way to bring in God's kingdom. Others have acted politically to protect the innocent and fight for human rights of the oppressed.

5. A SIMPLE CONFESSION OF FAITH.

From Matthew 16:16 came the cornerstone question for church membership: "Do you believe that Jesus is the Christ and accept him as your Lord and Savior?" Answering yes to that question is all that is required for membership. This simple question avoided the use of often-divisive creeds. Where many today will not make use of creeds; others will use them as a means of expressing faith—but not a test of faith. One of the early mottos of the movement that still has influence is "No creed but Christ."

6. BELIEVERS' BAPTISM.

Only people who have reached an age where they can make their own confession of faith are baptized, and the means of baptism is always immersion. Many congregations will accept into membership those who become church members through other traditions; other congregations are adamant that believers' baptism is essential. Baptisteries for immersion are features of worship facilities.

Baptism at Southeast Christian Church

167

7. WEEKLY COMMUNION.

Believing that the Lord's Supper is a vital experience of Jesus Christ, Stone-Campbell churches take Communion each Sunday. Some understand the Supper more as memorial while others see a real spiritual presence of Christ in it. Most invite all believers to the Table—both as a symbol and a promise of unity in Christ.

8. CONGREGATIONAL LEADERSHIP.

Most churches in this movement have no official organization beyond the local congregation, although they cooperate through many para-church organizations. Others are organized in regions or nationally but still with an emphasis on local congregational leadership. The "priesthood of all believers" is a mark of these churches. Participation by lay people in all aspects of the church's life is a notable feature, with many making no distinction between clergy and laity. Lay people conduct the sacraments. Women and men are seen as equal by many parts of the family but others see distinct roles for men and women.

9. FREEDOM AND DIVERSITY.

"In essentials unity, in nonessentials liberty, and in all things love" is one of the best-known slogans in our family. The Stone-Campbell Movement has always been characterized by an enriching diversity. Yet diversity also raises the potential of intolerance and division, and that, unfortunately, has also been part of our experience. This Christian family is left with the challenge of finding the unity-in-diversity that brought it into being over two hundred years ago as it seeks for the visible unity of the whole church of Jesus Christ.

MOVING INTO GOD'S FUTURE

What does the future hold for the Stone-Campbell Movement? The way we frame the question is important. "What does the future hold?" sounds as if we are in the hands of an uncontrollable fate. Perhaps we should ask, "What direction should our churches follow in the future?" But that question places too much faith in our human ability to discern the right path. "What does God want his church

Preaching

to be?" is the proper question. We know he holds the future. What we hope and pray for is discernment to see his hand at work and a willingness to submit to his will.

The authors do not claim to be prophets who know the future. However, we do pray for discernment and wisdom for the future direction of the Stone-Campbell Movement and the whole of God's church and God's world. In light of the heritage we briefly sketched above, we believe God is leading us in the following directions.

THE BIBLE FOR HEAD AND HEART

The future must be more than an institutional pilgrimage; it must be a spiritual one. Our past has sometimes focused on convincing the head instead of turning the heart. Both are needed. We want to have right doctrine, because we want to obey our Father, but doctrine must translate into life. Too many times we have been content with restoring the structure of the church and have neglected the weightier matters of justice, mercy, and faithfulness.

Ideally, one leads to the other. When Alexander Campbell penned his series of articles "On the Restoration of the Ancient Order of Things," his dream was that the restoration of the weekly

Lord's Supper, believer's immersion, and local church leadership would lead to a more spiritually disciplined church. It was not doctrine for doctrine's sake because he and our other early leaders objected to "cold orthodoxy." Instead, the Lord's Supper each week was to be a spiritual feast and an experiential participation in the death of Jesus. Baptism was to bring a heart-felt assurance of salvation and reconciliation. Appointing elders was not simply to be "organized correctly," but so that deeply spiritual leaders could guide others to a more intimate relation with Jesus.

A unity Movement needs the challenge, the comfort, and the assurance brought by the spiritual disciplines. In the words of *The Last Will and Testament of the Springfield Presbytery*, we should "pray more and dispute less." There are signs of spiritual renewal among us. We must restore and cultivate that spirituality sent by the Holy Spirit of God if we are truly to be the church Christ intends.

LORD, COME QUICKLY

The one certainty of the future is that our Lord will come again. We have at times neglected and misunderstood this truth. Alexander Campbell and others believed we could hasten the coming of Christ by uniting the church. Unfortunately, that millennial hope soon merged with the glorious future of the American republic. Campbell and others soon confused the success of America with the coming of the kingdom.

Later in our history, some forced premillennial Christians into their own congregations. Consequently, we neglected the book of Revelation and the anticipation of the Second Coming. We didn't talk much of the return of Jesus. We didn't know how he would return. Some assumed the kingdom had come in its fullness in the church, so we did not anticipate the culmination of the kingdom's coming at the end of time.

We are not suggesting it would be healthy to reopen the old postmillennial or premillennial or amillennial discussions. What we do need is a global kingdom vision. Jesus will return to bring a new heaven and new earth where God's will is done and justice and peace reign. All we do as a church we do in anticipation of that day. Indeed our value as a Restoration movement is completely based on God's promise to renew the heavens and the earth. We cannot as individuals or as a church constantly keep the Second Coming foremost in our minds (although we should think and speak of it more frequently). What we can do is be ready for his coming through constant faithful service.

The Second Coming relativizes all our plans and programs. It reminds us that God alone reigns, although now we only see that reign by faith. If our path is a journey, not a destination, we must also remember that we have a destination. Our pilgrimage is toward the New Jerusalem. This Stone-Campbell Movement ideally is precisely that, a journey to the heart of God. We must learn again to desire him alone—to look forward to that day when Jesus comes and we see God face to face.

May he come quickly.

QUESTIONS FOR DISCUSSION

1. In your experience does the Stone-Campbell Movement exhibit the nine characteristics listed above? What would you add to that list? What would you question?

2. What are some concrete ways we can work for Christian unity?

3. How does the mission of the church affect how we treat those of other cultures?

4. How have we sometimes ignored the urgency of the Second Coming of Jesus? How can we recover that urgency? How would it affect us as a church?

5. What evidence do you see of a spiritual awakening in the Stone-Campbell Movement?

6. What would you like for the Stone-Campbell Movement to become in the next twenty years?

FOR FURTHER READING

Williams, Newell, Douglas Foster, and Paul Blowers. *The Stone-Campbell Movement: A Global History* St. Louis, Missouri: Chalice 2013. See pages 367–381.

Website
World Convention. http://www.worldconvention.org/.

Study Guide

General Comments on Teaching a History of the Stone-Campbell Movement

1 This study guide is for small groups or church classes. It assumes that each student or family has a copy of the book and has read the appropriate chapter before the class meets.

2 Some Christians do not see a need for studying church history and may even see it as negative. There are many reasons for this. Some resist the idea that their church has been shaped by the ideas and events of their past, seeing their origins only in scripture. The first part of chapter one responds to such objections

3 Goals for the study of this history of the Stone-Campbell Movement include:

  a. To help members of churches from the Stone-Campbell Movement understand more fully how they have been shaped by the people, ideas, and events of the past, especially the last two hundred years.

  b. To explain and demonstrate the ideals that gave rise to the Stone-Campbell Movement in the nineteenth century and what we might draw from this heritage to strengthen our churches today.

  c. To examine and evaluate the parts of our history that have been detrimental to our spiritual health so we might be humbled and strive for a more Christ-like existence.

  d. To learn something about the 20th-century global expansion of the Stone-Campbell Movement that has resulted in the majority of churches and members being in the global south.

4 The material in each chapter focuses on one main idea and has been kept to as manageable a level in both length and complexity as possible. Teachers may feel a need to do other background reading on each topic. The "For Further Reading" section at the end of each chapter lists materials that deal specifically with the subject matter for that chapter. If you want to add three or four key books to your library that will consistently be helpful in this study, the following are ideal:

> Leroy Garrett, *The Stone-Campbell Movement*, College Press, 1994.
> Douglas A. Foster, et. al., *Encyclopedia of the Stone-Campbell Movement*, Eerdmans, 2005.
> Richard Hughes, *Reviving the Ancient Faith*, ACU Press, 2008.
> D. Newell Williams, Douglas A. Foster, and Paul M. Blowers, *The Stone-Campbell Movement, A Global History*. Chalice, 2013.

5 This study is not merely to learn historical facts, but to help shape us more into the likeness of Christ. Church historian Justo Gonzalez has said: "Every renewal of the church, every great age in its history, has been grounded on a renewed reading of history." Pray that this study will be part of a process of spiritual formation that will renew and revitalize this church and Christ's church throughout the world.

CHAPTER ONE: The Promise of Restoration in Early America

Teaching/ learning goals for this lesson include:

a. Point out and discuss ways the American background to the Stone-Campbell Movement helped shape it.
b. Develop an appreciation for the contributions of Smith, Jones, and O'Kelly to the Stone-Campbell Movement worldwide.
c. Identify strengths and weaknesses of the ideas and attitudes we have inherited.

Lesson Plan

1. Begin by reading Galatians 5:13-15. Follow with a prayer that we might live in freedom yet use that freedom to love our neighbors.
2. Chapter One focuses on the new religious situation that existed in America. All the religious bodies from Europe were transplanted to the "new world." Three important themes transformed these European influences: freedom, religious authority, and restoration. **Group Discussion:** What did "**freedom**" (or liberty) mean when it was applied to religion in America? What did religious people want to be free from?

174

3. One thing people wanted to be free from was the old religious **authorities**. Many did not want anyone telling them what to believe or practice—they could read the Bible and understand it for themselves. **Group Discussion:** What are the positive aspects of this attitude? When accompanied by a strong individualism and confidence in human reason, what are the potential dangers in this attitude?

4. The idea of **restoration** implies that something has deteriorated or been altered to the point that it is not what it could be or ought to be. **Group Discussion:** What aspects of Christianity did the leaders in this chapter believe needed to be restored in the 1800s? What aspects do you think need restoration today?

5. Two groups with roots in the American scene are the James O'Kelly Christians who broke with the Methodist Church, and the Elias Smith and Abner Jones Christians who broke with New England Baptists. **Group Discussion:** How do both of these groups reflect the three attitudes that characterized American Christianity? In what ways are these two groups different from one another? In what ways are these groups like your church in their beliefs, attitudes, and practices?

6. Close the class, if there is time, by asking each class member to jot down what he or she thought was the most important insight gained from the lesson. Ask for two or three hands of people who have not yet spoken aloud in class.

7. Close with prayer that God will use this study to shape us more into his likeness.

CHAPTER TWO: Barton Stone and Christian Unity

The teaching/ learning goals for this lesson include:

a. Describe the main events of the life of Barton W. Stone and his significance for the formation of the Stone-Campbell Movement.

b. Examine and analyze the events of the Cane Ridge meeting of August 1801 and the implications they had for the development of the movement.

c. Discuss the "Last Will and Testament of the Springfield Presbytery" and how these ideas have shaped the Stone-Campbell Movement.

Lesson Plan

1. Begin by reading Ephesians 4:2-6 and 11-16. Follow the reading by a prayer that we might have a deep commitment to maintaining the unity of the Spirit in the bond of peace, as did Barton W. Stone.

2. **Group Discussion:** Ask for three or four hands of people who can tell one fact about the early life of Barton W. Stone

3. **Group Discussion:** Why is it significant that Stone's religious training was at a Presbyterian school?

4. The Cane Ridge meeting was one of the most important events in what many historians call the "Second Great Awakening." Chapter two has a section describing the strange happenings at Cane Ridge and Stone's interpretation of them. **Group Discussion:** How do you understand what happened at the Cane Ridge meeting in August 1801? After three minutes, ask for three hands of persons who have not yet spoken to the whole class to report on what was said in their discussion.

5. Stone and the other Presbyterian ministers who helped with the Cane Ridge meeting got in trouble with the Synod of Kentucky (the Presbyterian body that was over them). The Synod of Kentucky was made up mostly of "Old Light" ministers who insisted on strict subscription to the Westminster Confession and denied that God used revivals to convert people. **Group Discussion: What would the members of the Synod of Kentucky have believed was wrong in what happened at Cane Ridge?**

6. In 1803, Stone and four other ministers formed their own Presbyterian body—the Springfield Presbytery. Yet by June of the following year, they dissolved that body and committed to be simply Christians, writing "The Last Will and Testament of the Springfield Presbytery," to explain their commitment. **Group Discussion:** Give the class four minutes to read the "Last Will and Testament" (it is contained in its entirety in the book). Ask them as they read to mark phrases that sound familiar to what they have heard before in their church. Also, ask them to mark any parts of the document that have NOT been part of their experience. Ask for four or five participants to tell one thing they marked that was familiar and one that was unfamiliar. Discuss these things.

7. Close with a prayer giving thanks for the godly example of Barton W. Stone who risked his livelihood and well being to work for the visible unity of Christ's church.

CHAPTER THREE: The Coming of the Campbells

The teaching/ learning goals for this lesson include

  a. Examine and evaluate the ideas of Thomas Campbell in his *Declaration and Address of the Christian Association.*
  b. Identify and analyze important life experiences of the Campbells that led them to begin their effort to reform the church.
  c. Discuss the relationship the Campbell churches had to the Baptist Associations.

Lesson Plan

1. Begin by reading John 13:34-35 and 15:5-8. Follow the reading by a prayer that we might have the desire truly to be disciples of Christ as did Thomas and Alexander Campbell.

2. The Campbells were from Northern Ireland. They lived in the midst of religious and political antagonism between Protestants and Catholics, British and Irish. Furthermore, as members of the Church of Scotland, which was Presbyterian, they had to deal with a number of internal disputes. Each faction denounced the others, refusing to worship together or even to recognize the others as Christians. **Group Discussion:** In groups of two or three, ask students to discuss for four minutes instances of religious conflict they have personally experienced or that they know about. After time is up, ask for three volunteers to briefly relate their experience. Then ask for three others to answer the question, "What is at the heart of these religious conflicts?"

3. Thomas Campbell came to America in 1807 and was assigned to preach in western Pennsylvania near Pittsburgh. When he served communion to Presbyterians not part of his faction, however, he got into trouble with the Synod, which within two years expelled him. He formed, with the help of people who supported him in western Pennsylvania, an association to promote simple "evangelical" Christianity and the unity of the church. Campbell was commissioned to write a document to explain the group's purpose. **Group Discussion:** Make a copy for every member of the class of the two-page list of Campbell's "Thirteen Propositions" that are part of the *Declaration and Address.* Hand these out and give the class members four minutes to read the document individually. Ask them as they read to mark phrases that sound familiar to what

they have heard before in their church. Also, ask them to mark any parts of the document that have NOT been part of their experience in their church. Ask for four or five hands to tell one thing they marked that was familiar and one that was unfamiliar. Discuss these things.

4. **Group Discussion:** Compare what you see in this small part of the *Declaration and Address* with what you saw last week in the "Last Will and Testament." What is the same? What is different?

5. **Group Discussion.** Discuss Alexander Campbell's views on the possibility of unimmersed persons being saved. What do you think his point really was? Why did he say the things he did when he was a very strong proponent of believers' immersion—even to the point of refusing anyone who was not immersed membership in the churches of his reform movement?

6. Close the class with a prayer of thanksgiving for the passion and courage of the Campbells to work for the unity and purity of Christ's church, and that we might also have that passion and courage today.

CHAPTER FOUR: The Stone and Campbell Movements Unite

The teaching/ learning goals for this lesson include:

a. Compare and contrast the ideas and beliefs of Barton W. Stone and Alexander Campbell and their movements.

b. Describe how many of the churches of the two movements united, creating one of the largest religious reform movements in America.

c. Discuss how they were able to unite despite significant differences and what implications there might be in this event for churches today.

Lesson Plan

1. Begin by reading Colossians 3:12-15. Follow the reading by a prayer that Christians would bear with one another in love as the members of the Stone and Campbell movements did when they united with each other to glorify God and strengthen His kingdom.

2. **Group Discussion.** The teacher should write out the seven classical categories of doctrine: God, Christ, Holy Spirit, Humanity,

Salvation, Church, and Last Things/ End of Time. Then, ask class members as individuals to write out as many doctrinal differences in these categories between Barton W. Stone and Alexander Campbell that they can think of in the next three or four minutes. Tell them they can consult their books. After doing this as individuals, have them read their lists to one another in groups of two or three. Finally, call the whole class back together. Write all the differences the class members identified. Try to do it by writing the differences in the doctrinal categories. **Group Discussion.** Again in groups of two and three, ask the groups to decide which of the differences was the most serious, and why.

3. The most famous early union of churches took place in late December 1831 and early January 1832 in Lexington, Kentucky. Read part of the account of the union, especially parts of the speech of Raccoon John Smith and the acceptance by Stone of the proposal for unity. **Group Discussion.** What allowed the two churches in Lexington to come together in December, 1831? Why didn't their differences prevent this from happening?

4. **Group Discussion.** Is the unity of Christ's church worth giving one's life to? What precisely might that commitment look like in the Stone-Campbell Movement today? In your congregation today?

5. Walter Scott began preaching what he called the *gospel restored* that could be made memorable by using five fingers to make his points (he started with six points—but five worked better): faith, repentance, baptism, forgiveness of sins, and the gift of the Holy Spirit. **Class Discussion:** Discuss the fervor for evangelism in Scott's time and since. How has it been healthy? Has it ever been problematic? Are the churches you know today still evangelistic?

6. The creation of the American Christian Missionary Society in 1849 was a milestone in the history of the Stone-Campbell Movement—some would say for good and others for bad. **Class Discussion:** Why did those who organized the American Christian Missionary Society believe it was needed? What objections might have been raised against the society? What is the significance of the society as far as what it says about the Movement?

7. Close the class with a prayer of thanksgiving for the example of those in our heritage who were committed to the visible unity of Christ's church, and asking for wisdom and discernment for how

we can reflect in our circumstances today the truth that there is one body. Also pray that God will again give this Movement a zeal for evangelism and the growth of Christ's church and kingdom.

CHAPTER FIVE: The Great Divide of the American Civil War

Teaching/ learning goals for this lesson include:

   a. Examine ways the sectionalism of the American Civil War and the accompanying racial attitudes shaped the Stone-Campbell Movement in America and elsewhere.
   b. Explain the role of the American Civil War and sectionalism in the divisive issues of missionary societies and instrumental music in worship.
   c. Discuss the relation of the Christian to politics and war.

Lesson Plan

1. Begin by reading from Jesus' prayer for his followers in John 17:15-16. Follow the reading by a prayer that we will increasingly understand what it means not to be "of the world" as we reflect Christ's mission and not the world's values and actions.
2. Do a mini-lecture on the section titled "Slavery, Race, and the Churches." **Group Discussion.** Then, ask the class in groups of two or three to discuss **why** the churches and leaders of the Stone-Campbell Movement took the positions they did regarding slavery. Give them four minutes. Ask for three volunteers who will briefly report on the main idea discussed in their group.

The point of this exercise is to reveal how powerfully the surrounding culture affects the thought and actions of the church. Slavery was an accepted way of life for many Americans; some today may even be able to argue like James Shannon that scripture does not condemn slavery; it only seeks to regulate slavery for the "benefit" of the black race (usually seen as inherently inferior). This reflects a certain view of the nature of scripture. If one sees the Bible **primarily** as a book of facts to be handled in a legalistic manner, one can certainly defend slavery with scripture. If one sees scripture **primarily** as the living, active word of God, the sword of the Spirit, which takes hold of our hearts and minds and shapes us into the likeness of Christ, then the practice of the owning of human beings will be seen for the inherently immoral practice it is and rejected by the church and Christians.

3. **Group Discussion.** Discuss how the American Christian Missionary Society served as a divisive institution in the Stone-Campbell Movement because of the events of the Civil War. While there were some who objected to the missionary society for various reasons, it did not become an issue that divided churches until after the Civil War. Point out that even some of the society's staunchest opponents like Tolbert Fanning had refused to allow it to become a point of division until the Civil War events. **What are the implications of these facts?**

4. **Group Discussion.** Invite the class to evaluate the positions of Daniel Sommer and T. B. Larimore. For example, you might divide the class into groups of four or five and have them discuss and write out the strongest defense of their assigned person. If you had to defend Daniel Sommer to a hostile crowd, how would you do it? If you had to defend T. B. Larimore to a hostile crowd, how would you do it? Allow five or six minutes for the discussion and writing of the defense. Monitor the groups and call time when it appears most have finished their assignment. Then choose a spokesperson from each "side" to come up to the front to defend Sommer and Larimore. Finally, open up a full class discussion on what they see as fundamentally at stake in the late nineteenth century concerning the unity of the Movement and the understanding of what the church really is.

5. **Group Discussion.** Discuss how doctrinal issues are never simply doctrinal issues. Future lessons will make the point that many in the Stone-Campbell Movement are now being forced to reexamine their identity. As we understand better the ways we have been profoundly shaped by cultural issues, we are equipped to see where that has sometimes been a detriment to our fulfilling God's intent for his church.

6. Close class with a prayer that the spirit of division be removed from our hearts.

CHAPTER SIX: The Christian Church (Disciples of Christ)

Teaching/ learning goals for this lesson include:

a. Describe the development of church structure among the Disciples, particularly as it relates to their conventions, missionary societies, and finances.

b. Discuss the tensions that accompany these developments.

181

c. Explain the new theologies of both mission and church that emerged among Disciples.

d. Examine the ecumenical work of the Christian Church (Disciples of Christ)

e. Discuss the current challenges Disciples face in their church life and their responses to those challenges.

Lesson Plan

1. Begin by reading 1 Corinthians 10:14-17. Follow the reading with a prayer for greater insight into the truths that we welcome all to the Lord's Table as God has welcomed us, so that we might participate in God's reconciliation of the world.

2. **Group Discussion.** In what ways did rapid growth and the desire to be effective in mission lead Disciples to create new ways of being church together? What kind of challenges arose from those developments? Is organization a blessing or a curse for the church?

3. Work for Christian unity is a consistent value of Disciples. **Group Discussion.** What do we mean when we describe unity as "a gift of God's grace"? How does this relate to our understanding that "divisions are caused by human beings"?

4. The growth of ethnic congregations has been a major factor in the increasing vitality of Disciples life in the last twenty years, **Group Discussion:** discuss in groups of four or five the history of your congregation in light of the material in the chapter concerning the vitality of ethnic congregations. Then come together as a class to discuss how you might connect your congregation's ministries to those of other congregations in your city as a model of how diverse churches can work together in mission.

5. Talk about the numerical decline of Disciples since the 1960s. **Group Discussion:** What factors have caused this decline? What might be a recipe for turning things around? What initiatives have been proposed to respond to the current context?

6. Close the class time with a prayer of thanksgiving for those who have gone before us, who gave their lives to teach the gospel and establish churches, even in the midst of imperfect understandings. Ask that we be given godly understandings of who we are and what we should do, yet that we also be blessed in our flawed understandings as we give our hearts and lives to the service of Christ.

CHAPTER SEVEN: Christian Churches and Churches of Christ
Teaching/ learning goals for this lesson include:

   a. Examine how Christian Churches/Churches of Christ came to
   have a distinct identity in the Stone-Campbell Movement.
   b. Describe how Christian Churches/Churches of Christ developed structure for cooperating in life and mission.
   c. Discuss the reasons for growth of Christian Churches/
   Churches of Christ.

Lesson Plan

1. Begin by reading Matthew 28:18-20. Follow the reading with a
   prayer that God will lead our churches into ways of making disciples in every nation.
2. From 1950 to 1990, Christian Churches/Churches of Christ ener-
   getically gave rise to the work of missions, evangelism, education,
   campus ministries, and conventions. **Group Discussion:** In
   groups of three, assess the impact of this work: what programs
   and organizations were most effective? Which ones best manifest
   the character of this stream of the Stone-Campbell Movement?
   What structures give these churches a group identity? Have one
   from each group report on their discussion.
3. **Group Discussion.** Discuss the three approaches or mindsets
   among Christian Churches/Churches of Christ described in this
   chapter—conservative restorationists, evangelicals, and a free
   church approach. Are these accurate descriptions of diversity? In
   what other ways are those in Christian Churches/Churches of
   Christ diverse?
4. Christian Churches/ Churches of Christ are often listed as being
   one of the fastest growing churches on the United States. **Group
   Discussion:** Have the class in groups of two or three decide on
   what they believe is the single most important factor in that
   growth. Give them about four minutes to discuss. Ask for three
   hands to tell what they thought was most important and why.
   There is no right or wrong answer—there is a complicated set of
   interwoven circumstances that contributed.
5. Close with a prayer that we might grow in our discernment of the
   true nature of the Lord's church and toward a maturity in Christ
   that enables us to serve others.

CHAPTER EIGHT: Churches of Christ

Teaching/ learning goals for this lesson include:

a. Examine the changing hermeneutic of Churches of Christ and the part it played in creating a self-identity.

b. Describe racism in Churches of Christ, historically and in the churches today.

c. Discuss how the self-identity of Churches of Christ is changing today.

Lesson Plan

1. Begin by reading 1 Peter 2:21-25. Follow the reading with a prayer that our identity as a church will be centered on being Christ to others—that is, being willing to give ourselves for the sake of others; and not merely on having the "right" structures or in saying the "right" things.

2. Ask the class for a definition of "hermeneutics." Then ask if they remember what the "old hermeneutic" was for much of the twentieth century (command, example, inference). The book suggests that the "silence of scripture" was a key part of our understanding of how to interpret the Bible. **Group Discussion:** Ask the class to discuss in groups of two or three what they believe the significance of the silence of scripture to be—in other words, if the scripture neither commands nor prohibits a thing, what does that mean about whether or not that thing can be practiced? Give them four minutes, and then ask for three hands. This question was important in many periods of the church's history. One position insists that the silence of scripture prohibits—if it doesn't say do it, you can't do it. The other position says that if something is not mentioned, it might be used if it is in keeping with the spirit of scripture and builds up the church. Which position on the silence of scripture do you see most often in Churches of Christ today? Which do you think is more in keeping with God's will? Why?

3. Talk about the expansion of African American Churches of Christ due to the tireless evangelism of Bowser, Keeble, and other preachers. **Group Discussion:** What was the difference between the work of Bowser and Keeble? Why was there a difference? Which do you think was more godly in his approach to white racism? Churches of Christ generally succumbed to the racism and segregation that was part of American culture through most

of its history. **Group Discussion:** Ask the question, why did Churches of Christ maintain segregated churches and practice discrimination during most of our existence? Was it right? Are Churches of Christ still largely segregated?

4. **Group Discussion:** "The loss of self-assurance among many of us in Churches of Christ has led to an increased awareness of our dependence on God and on the guidance of his Spirit." After reading this statement from the book to the class, ask them to think for a moment and respond from the perspective of their own congregation, either disagreeing or agreeing, and telling why.

5. **Group Discussion:** Close the lesson with a discussion on whether or not the diversity in Churches of Christ today, in contrast to the uniformity of fifty years ago, is mostly a plus or a minus. The reality of the diversity and the increased options churches seem to have cannot be denied—yet this has made the uncertainty and "identity crisis" in Churches of Christ even sharper.

6. Close the class with a prayer that we find our identity in Christ and in being Christ to those who surround us.

CHAPTER NINE: Britain, The Commonwealth And Europe

Teaching/ learning goals for this lesson include:

a. Describe the rise of the Stone-Campbell Movement in Great Britain, noticing the different roots and emphases from the Movement in America.

b. Describe influential leaders in these places.

c. Discuss what the Stone-Campbell Movement in these places looks like today.

Lesson Plan

1. Begin by reading Acts 17:16-34. Follow with a prayer that we might have wisdom on how to speak the good news into a Western secular society.

2. Ask any group members who have visited or lived in Great Britain, Canada, Australia, New Zealand, or Europe to tell of their experiences there. Did they attend church there? What was that like?

3. Churches in Great Britain were influenced by the early writings of Alexander Campbell with little influence from Barton Stone: **Group Discussion:** From what the class remembers about the

185

differences between Stone and Campbell, they should discuss how the emphases of Campbell particularly shaped the Stone-Campbell Movement in Great Britain and the Commonwealth.

4. **Group Discussion:** Discuss the influence of the following leaders: David King in England, A.L. Haddon in New Zealand, and A.R. Main in Australia. What made them influential? What kind of ministries did they have? What does this tell us about the Stone-Campbell Movement?

5. In Russia and in Spain, Christian movements began independently of the Stone-Campbell movement but eventually joined it. **Group Discussion:** In groups of 3-4, discuss why you think that groups developed similar ideas to the Stone-Campbell Movement. Then, let one member of each group share his or her answers with the entire group.

6. **Group Discussion:** Why has it been difficult for Stone-Campbell churches to grow numerically in Europe? What might be done to promote more numerical growth?

7. End class with a prayer for the people, churches and Christians in Great Britain, Canada, Australia, New Zealand, and Europe.

CHAPTER TEN: Asia and the Pacific Islands

Teaching/ learning goals for this lesson include:

a. Describe how the Stone-Campbell Movement entered Asia and the Pacific.
b. Examine the missionary approaches taken in these countries.
c. Reflect on particular emphases of the churches in these countries.
d. Discuss what the Stone-Campbell Movement in these places looks like today.

Lesson Plan

1. Read Acts 2:42-47. Then pray that we might be as devoted a church as this first church in Asia was.

2. **Group Discussion:** Begin by asking the group what first comes to their minds when they think of "Asia." Then, ask any group members who have visited or lived in Asia or the Pacific Islands to tell of their experiences there. Did they attend church there? What was that like?

3. In addition to planting churches, missionaries in Asia also began schools, clinics, publishing houses, and orphanages. **Group Discussion:** Why did they spend time and resources on these organizations instead of simply planting churches? What does this say about their view of mission and evangelism?
4. From reading this chapter, it appears that women were more active on the "mission field" than they were generally in the sending churches in the United States, Great Britain, Australia, and New Zealand. **Group Discussion:** Why did women have more of a leadership role in missions? Again, what does this say about the view of mission and evangelism of these international workers?
5. In Korea and other Asian countries, there seems to be more emphasis on group prayer than is found in many of the Stone-Campbell churches in the West. **Group Discussion:** Why might this be? What does it say about Western Christianity?
6. Missionaries have been sent from these countries to many others. **Group Discussion:** Discuss our notions of missionary sending countries and missionary receiving countries. How are those concepts changing?
7. End class with a prayer for the peoples, churches and Christians in Asia and the Pacific Islands.

CHAPTER ELEVEN: The Caribbean and Latin America
Teaching/ learning goals for this lesson include:

a. Describe how the Stone-Campbell Movement entered the Caribbean and Latin America.
b. Examine the missionary approaches taken in these countries.
c. Reflect on particular emphases of the churches in these countries.
d. Discuss what the Stone-Campbell Movement in these places looks like today.

Lesson Plan

1. Read Acts 10:34-48. Pray that we will follow the God who does not show favoritism but accepts those of every nation.
2. **Group Discussion:** Begin by asking the group what first comes to their minds when they think of "Latin America." Of the Caribbean? Then ask any group members who have visited or

lived in Latin America or the Caribbean to tell of their experiences there. Did they attend church there? What was that like?

3. After the Revival of 1933, the Christian Church (Disciples of Christ) in Puerto Rico has been heavily influenced by Pentecostal practices that are not found in most Stone-Campbell churches worldwide. **Group Discussion:** In groups of two or three, share your own experience with Pentecostal or charismatic practices. Then discuss whether those practices (or others) should be matters of fellowship among Christians. After the groups report to the entire class, have a class discussion of how the Stone-Campbell Movement can be unified even with a variety of practices and beliefs.

4. Several para-church organizations like the Pan American Lectureship, Great Cities Missions, Predisan, and Christian Missionary Fellowship have promoted church planting and medical missions in Latin America. **Group Discussion:** Is the work of these organizations different from the work of earlier Missionary Societies or of Global Ministries of the Christian Church (Disciples of Christ)? If so, in what way are they different? What has been the effect of these organizations on Stone-Campbell churches in Latin America?

5. Latin America was one of the first places that American churches sent large mission teams instead of a few individuals or families. **Group Discussion:** What are the advantages of large teams? Disadvantages?

6. For several decades, the Christian Church (Disciples of Christ) has worked with existing denominations and ecumenical organizations instead of planting new churches internationally. Churches of Christ and Christian Churches/Churches of Christ have focused on planting new congregations and have not generally partnered with ecumenical organizations. **Group Discussion:** Why have the groups taken different approaches in their missions? What could each approach learn from the other?

7. End class with a prayer for the peoples, churches and Christians of Latin America and the Caribbean.

CHAPTER TWELVE: Africa, the New Center of Christianity

Teaching/ learning goals for this lesson include:

a. Describe how the Stone-Campbell Movement entered Africa.
b. Examine the missionary approaches taken in these countries.
c. Reflect on particular emphases of the churches in these countries.
d. Discuss what the Stone-Campbell Movement in these places looks like today.

Lesson Plan

1. Read Acts 8:26-39. Pray that we will have the same heart to obey God as this African had.

2. **Group Discussion:** Begin by asking the group what first comes to their minds when they think of "Africa." Then ask any group members who have visited or lived Africa to tell of their experiences there. Did they attend church there? What was that like? Did that experience or something in this chapter help dispel some stereotypes and give a clearer view of Africa?

3. This chapter calls Africa the new center of Christianity because of the rapid growth of churches there. **Group Discussion:** Why do you think these churches are growing so rapidly in Africa? What are some implications of the numerical strength of African Christianity for Christianity worldwide? For the Stone-Campbell Movement?

4. In many of these countries in recent decades, mission has shifted from direct church planting by missionaries from other countries to training indigenous evangelists through schools. **Group Discussion:** Is this a healthy shift? What long-term effects might it have? Does this shift have implications for what we mean by "gospel," "evangelism," and "mission."

5. The chapter mentions several Pan African gatherings to promote evangelism. **Group Discussion:** Why might it be difficult for African church leaders from different countries to work together? What does it say about "missions" when Africans are taking on the responsibility of evangelizing Africa and the rest of the world? What can Christians in other places learn from this?

6. End class with a prayer for the peoples, churches and Christians of Africa.

CHAPTER 13: A Global Movement Faces the Future

Teaching/ learning goals for this lesson include:

a. Discuss understandings of the term "missionary" to examine the ways our churches can become "missional" in their understanding of their identity.

b. Analyze the common characteristics of our churches worldwide.

c. Reflect on the blessings God has given to the Stone-Campbell Movement and the direction God might be leading us.

Lesson Plan

1. Begin by reading Hebrews 13:11-16. Follow the reading with a prayer that we will not be complacent in our Christian journey, thinking that we have arrived. Rather, that we will see ourselves as refugees, seeking the lasting city that is to come.

2. This chapter describes past and current mission work this way: The usual pattern was for countries to send out missionaries who would evangelize, then train local leaders, eventually leading to indigenous churches independent of but still in fellowship with the churches of the sending country. Today, the view of mission is a **partnership** between sending and receiving churches. Few missionaries see themselves as "running a mission" but rather as assisting local leaders in spreading the Good News through proclamation, education, medical assistance, agricultural instruction, and economic justice. **Group Discussion:** Do a quick word association exercise. Ask each class member to write down as many words or phrases that come to mind when you say the word "missionary". Give them only twenty seconds. Then ask them to call out words they wrote. As you record these answers, put the responses that are negative on the left, positive on the right, neutral in the middle. After about a minute of responses, see how many negatives there are as compared to positives or neutrals. Do the same with the word, "partner." Many Americans see "missionary" as mostly a negative word. Why? Why would Christians want to be missionaries?

3. List the nine common characteristics of our churches-- concern for Christian unity, commitment to evangelism and mission, an emphasis on Scripture, a call to peace and justice, a simple confession of faith, believers' baptism, weekly communion,

190

congregational leadership, and freedom and diversity. **Group Discussion:** Would you see some of these as more important than others? Which of these might you say is most important? Which is most characteristic of our churches? Which do we need to cultivate more?

4. The church is a "House of prayer for all the nations." **Group Discussion**: Talk about what you think that means for the way we live our lives as Christians and congregations. In what ways have we been this? In what ways have we failed? In what ways can we be that? What are specific ways your congregation is embracing the poor, the sick, the powerless and rejecting the dream of success for religious organizations?

5. **Group Discussion:** What evidences of spiritual renewal can you see in Stone-Campbell Churches generally and in your congregation today? In what ways do you think this will change the way our congregations look and operate?

6. Close the class and the series with a time of prayer. Allow anyone who wants to voice a thanksgiving for our heritage, a petition for the growth of Christ's kingdom, or other requests for renewal, etc. to do so briefly. Spend, if possible, at least five minutes in prayer this way. There may be times of silence. Close the prayer by asking God that this study bless those who participated and result in our being formed more into the likeness of Christ.

Printed in the USA
CPSIA information can be obtained
at www.ICGtesting.com
LVHW042331180823
755636LV00005B/505

9 780891 123736